GREEN CAPITALISM
Manufacturing Scarcity in an Age of Abundance

James Heartfield

For Daisy Heartfield, may she want for nothing

I owe a great deal to Ian Abley, Ron Arnold, Daniel Ben-Ami, J.J. Charlesworth, Rob Clowes, Wendell Cox, Phil Cunliffe, Ceri Dingle, Neil Davenport, Paul Dreisson, Martin Durkin, the late Dave Hallsworth, Frank Furedi, Alex Gourevitch, Philip Hammond, Julie Hearn, Patrick Hughes, Solomon Hughes, Eve Kay, Kevin McCullagh, Peter Martin, Munira Mirza, Kate Moorcock, Phil Mullan, Brendan O'Neill, Michael Perelman, Peter Ramsay, Ben Seymour, Hillel Ticktin and James Woudhuysen – though whether any of them will agree with the arguments here is another thing.

Heartfield *Green Capitalism*

Contents

1. The Age of Plenty   5
    Capitalism and the industrial revolution   7
    Cornucopia   8
    Reinventing Scarcity in an Age of Abundance   10

2. The Contemporary Retreat from Production   12

3. The Green Capitalists   21
    The greenwashers   25
    The birth of green capitalism

4. Manufactured scarcity: the profits of deindustrialisation   33
    Carbon trading   34
    Clean energy and 'negawatts'   37
    Land retirement   40
    The 'green belt'   44

5. Green Consumerism   48
    Ethical shopping is status affirmation   49
    Organic foods   51
    Air travel   53
    The green consumer's dilemma   55

6. The Economy of wasting time   58
    Recycling   61
    Reversing the division of labour   62

7. Green Imperialism   67
    Setting limits on the developing world   70
    Indigenism   78
    Green Colonialism   82

8. Environmental Economics   83

9. Green Socialism? No thanks.   91
    Austerity socialism   91
    Green Marx?   93

10. The unnatural limits to economic growth   97

Appendix: The Revolution in Technique   99

Bibliography   121

Index   128

James Heartfield
www.heartfield.org

January 2008

The global elite is in the grip of a terrible nightmare. The nightmare is cornucopia. For the ruling classes nothing is more alarming than the steady rise in mass consumerism. Across the world they see the advance of consumer power as a drain on their precious resources. The age of plenty is an anathema to them. Superstores, cheap air travel, fat kids, suburban sprawl, and takeaway food fill them with dread. Their biggest fear is that the Chinese should take to driving cars. They dream instead of restoring strict limits on consumption. If scarcity is in danger of being overcome, their ambition is to artificially recreate it.

For thirty millennia mankind lived under the tyranny of scarcity. The struggle to survive dominated human experience. Perched on the edge of existence men were at the mercy of the elements. Droughts, famine, floods, and disease threatened extinction. We were slaves to the relentless cycles of night and day, high and low tide, summer and winter. The earth only gave up the means by which we survived, food, shelter, warmth, very grudgingly. Backbreaking toil has been the lot of the small farmer since men first settled the land.

Hardship stunted the moral and intellectual growth of men. Dominated by nature in fact, they were in thrall to phantoms in their imaginations. Superstitious in beliefs, custom bound in their social lives, ignorant intellectually – there was nothing virtuous about poverty.

Only by industry, by husbanding the soil, by honing the tools, by storing the grain, by re-routing the waters, gathering the wood, digging the coal, drilling the oil, smelting the iron and steel did men ever succeed in wresting more the earth than they needed. The surplus, over and above bare existence, is what makes us human.

But the surplus was for so long, small: little more than a grain store, a salted ham, a barrel of apples for the winter. More than nature needs was hard to come by.

Without enough to go around, all communal bonds, till now, have been little more than systems for rationing the surplus. Monasteries and castles, temples and parliaments, long-halls and pyramids – these are the monuments left by the great class wars over the surplus product that has raged for the last five thousand years. The prize to the victors: a life of plenty, amid squalor. Their civilisation was not much more than an armed stockade around the food store.

Freedom from necessity was so rare a commodity that it was concentrated in the hands of the privileged few. The leisured classes, whether aristocratic or priestly, warlord or capitalist have had to fight hard to defend their privileges. Subjugation of the toiling masses was the condition of the freedom of the elite. Human civilisation, whether literary or scientific, has blossomed in the free time won by the few, on the backs of many. Scarcity made the human order into a bitter war over social product.

Throughout human history, the powers-that-be have stood on the solid authority of scarcity. Ever since Joseph took control of the Pharoah's grain store, authority has meant rationing. Doling out the rations is the first function of all authority. Whether it was wages, or benefits, homes or health-care, the person in control of the rations has always been the one with the whip.

Capitalism was from the outset a system of rationing.

Capitalism rations scarce goods through the market mechanism. It disperses the weekly ration to families as wages. It recovers its costs by limiting access to goods. It reduces us to wage slaves by controlling access to the means of subsistence. Capitalism cannot exist without scarcity. Scarcity is capitalism's means of social control

But capitalism is also the system that has over time abolished scarcity. As well as a system of social control, capitalism is a system for producing goods. To create an ever-greater surplus, capitalism has revolutionised technology, so reducing costs. The profit system drove people to create abundance. In doing so capitalism has abolished the basis for its own control.

Industrial revolution

The industrial revolution turned the world upside down. Putting a premium on cutting wage costs, capitalism set in motion the single greatest transformation in human history. At last, here was a system that rewarded the abbreviation of working time: the factory system. Begun in 1721 at the Lombe Silk Works on the Derwent, the factory system has expanded to embrace the world. Greedily swallowing up labour power, the factory had to be reined in by trade unions and the law.

The gains of the factory system are straightforward. As it grew, output grew faster than the number of people. Result: happiness. In Britain between 1801 and 1911 the population grew from 10.5 million to 41.8 million, an annual increase of 1.25 per cent, while output grew by 2-2.25 per cent a year.[1] In the last century, world population grew more than it did in the previous 30,000 years. Happily, world output increased faster, so that output per head grew nearly ten times, from $679 to $6539 between 1900 and 2000.[2] Only because output grew faster is it possible that those more than four billion new people survive.

The history of technology is a subject in itself (see appendix, The Revolution in Technique). To abbreviate: levers, pulleys and then machines substituted for routine human tool-use; mills and dray animals, and then later engines substituted for human motive power; wood, coal, oil and gas substituted for dietary calories providing warmth, light and then, with machines, kinetic energy.

To do the same thing over and over again, said Heraclitus, is not just boredom, it is slavery. Technology, substituting for routine work can set us free. The division of labour made dull but efficient work out of mysterious craftsmanship. Once isolated, routine could be mechanised.

And because industry isolates the repetitive actions from the creative side of work, it is driven by standardisation. Modern technology levels, distilling the essence out in different circumstances.

---

[1] Paul Kennedy, *The Rise and Fall of the Great Powers,* London, Fontana, 1990, p.197
[2] 'Estimating World GDP' Brad DeLong, http://econ161.berkeley.edu/TCEH/1998_Draft/World_GDP/Estimating_World_GDP.html

It prefers purer energy sources like oil, and electricity because of their universality of application, to bulky and unpredictable wood, wind and coal.

Technology has tended to the development, not of the universal worker, the Robot, but to the universal machine, the computer, which substitutes more effectively for routines that lay far beyond the calculating capacities of people.

But for the elite cultural reaction against it, today's era would be known as the Age of Plastics, the universal construction materials that have freed our goods from the constraints of natural forms (at least at the super-molecular level).

Cornucopia

The future is here. We are largely free from the direct domination of nature. For most of us, absolute scarcity is a thing of the past – thanks to the revolution in technique.

The Worldwatch Institute estimated that 1.7 billion people earn enough to buy into the consumer society. It is true that only in West Europe and America, does the 'consumer class' approach to the whole population. But still 29 per cent of the consumer class, 494 million are in East Asia, a tenth in East Europe and another tenth in Latin America.[3]

In material terms there is no basis for scarcity today. Food output – despite the Reverend Malthus' fears – outstripped population. Good news for most of us.

But for some, the end of scarcity is an outrage. They cannot believe that people can enjoy the good life. For them, the very sight of other people eating, drinking, enjoying themselves is disgusting. The puritan ethos was a great thing, when Britons were faced with real scarcity, but some people do not know how to let it go.

But the demand for rationing is not just a cultural reaction. Controlling access to the means of subsistence has been the way that society was organised since the dawn of human settlements.

---

[3] Worldwatch Institute, *State of the World,* London, W. W. Norton, 2004, p 7

Scarcity was never just scarcity. It was also a weapon in the struggle to establish mastery. The bread-and-water diet, doling out the ship's biscuits, taxing peasants, land distribution, the ration-book, wage negotiations – these were the ways that the ruling class ruled.

The super-abundance generated by modern industry calls the authority of the powers-that-be into question.

Even modern capitalism – the system that developed industry – struggles to justify its profits in the face of super-abundance.

The natural tendency of prices is downwards, as productivity increases. More and more we see costs of reproduction pushed so low that they are getting close to negligible.

That is what happened to electronically reproduced music. Here were goods that you could take away, while leaving them there. The commodity-form of old coincided with finite goods, whose ownership implied they were denied to others.

Instantaneous reproduction at negligible cost threatens the very structure of private property relations. Increasingly, profits can only be generated through the artificial imposition of a legal title to payment for licensed use. Naturally enough, the dependence upon the law to enforce payments tempts teenagers to evade it.

You will not be able to download food from the internet in the foreseeable future, but here too, the same downward trend in costs is clear. UK households spent around one third of their income on food in 1950 and about one tenth today – thanks to the growth of factory farms that push down prices.

Government scientist Sir David King suggests that cheap and available food has helped make Britain overweight. Meanwhile Americans throw away one quarter of all their food uneaten, and the figure for Britain is a staggering 30-40 per cent[4] – modern consumers put little value on food. At the same time small farmers are leaving the industry, as returns shrink.

Modern industry is dissolving the artificial representation of output as discrete goods, with a price label, and laying bare its real character as a series of developing relationships.

---

[4] *Guardian* 15 April 2005

The growing importance of intellectual property rights is a sign that the propertied elite is losing touch with the world of production. Western copyright lawyers are hunting China's cities for an unearned share of their industry.

More and more capital is tied up in unproductive speculation. The financial wizards are increasingly preoccupied with securing future value streams independent of any kind of productive activity. Growth, whether in housing, dot.com companies or the fine art market, generally means asset inflation, without any corresponding increase in production. Indeed investors prefer goods whose supply is limited, rationed, like Britain's over-regulated housing market, or unique goods like fine art.

Reinventing Scarcity in an age of abundance

'Allow not nature more than nature needs, man's life's as cheap as beast's' Shakespeare, *King Lear,* Act II, Scene IV

In the face of real super-abundance, saving the rule of private property means reinventing scarcity. Artificially manufactured scarcity is the condition for the reimposition of capitalist authority.

The last nature-imposed famines were in India in the 1960s. The 'green revolution' that brought high-yield crops, fertilisers and motorisation put an end to India's recurrent famines.

Since then, famines have been man-made. Starvation in Cambodia came through a combination of American bombardment and Khmer Rouge depopulation of the cities. The 1986 Ethiopian famine was a product of war. Localised famines in inland Somalia were transformed into a general collapse in output once American agricultural surpluses dumped in Mogadishu as USAID pushed grain prices to zero, so that farmers abandoned their plots and invaded the port.

Economist Rehman Sobhan explained why the single greatest aid recipient, Bangladesh, was so poor: aid agencies were so numerous that they recruited all the most talented Bengalis away from fruitful work.

Man-made famines re-establish a new ruling order. Michael Maren described the way that aid agencies came to rule over the East African villages he worked in. Aid workers, often young people with precious little experience, lorded it over their black subjects.[5]

In the developed world, too, the enemies of abundance are struggling to reinvent scarcity.

Over and again experts have warned us that the exhaustion of natural resources is at hand. In every case, these warnings have proved false.

In the 1970s, we were warned that oil reserves were running out. But as prices increased those reserves were discovered to be many times greater than previously thought. Today, again we are being told that 'peak oil' is in sight. But these remain theoretical assertions without any justification.

Then we were warned about deforestation. But it turned out that in the United States forestland is growing 5886 square kilometres on average every year. In the European Union forests are growing 486 million cubic metres every year.[6]

Herbert Girardet warned us that our human footprint – the area of land needed to generate the goods we consume – was getting bigger, and soon the cities would consume the countryside. Now we know that the actual human footprint covers fewer acres each year, as grain yields per acre increase. In the United States, the human footprint (developed + farm land) has shrunk by 15 per cent since 1950.[7]

Paul Erhlich thought that the increase in population meant that there would be a generalised materials and goods famine by the mid 1980s. In fact food production outstripped household demand, as raw materials did industrial demand.

Inventing scarcity today takes a big leap of the imagination. Struggling to demonstrate shortages in an age of abundance, the scare-

---

[5] Michael Maren, *The Road to Hell,* New York, The Free Press, 1997; Julie Hearn, 'African NGOs: the new compradors?' *Development and Change,* Volume 38 Issue 6 Page 1095-1110, November 2007
[6] Office of National Statistics, *Britain 2000,* London, HMSO, p.463
[7] Wendell Cox, *War on the Dream,* Lincoln, iUniverse, 2006, p. 73

mongers have left the mundane world altogether and discovered a shortage in the ether.

Of course climate change is an important scientific question, but that is quite a different thing from the contemporary cultural interpretation of climate change as a coming catastrophe. Whether a warmer planet would mean more goods or less is a moot point. What is certain is that those who need to believe in scarcity will discover it in climate change. Climate change scare mongering is the final etherialisation of scarcity.

What needs to be explained is not the natural limits to growth. What needs to be explained is the determination in some quarters to believe, despite the evidence to the contrary, that we have reached the natural limits to growth.

The green capitalists' *a priori* belief in limits is independent of any empirical substantiation. It is the prejudice of an elite that can only exercise authority by controlling the rations. These are the prejudices that laid the basis for a new kind of capitalism – green capitalism. And the first stage in the genesis of green capitalism is the retreat from production.

DAFT PREDICTIONS OF THE GREENS

Climatologists are pessimistic that political leaders will take any positive actions to compensate for climate change ...The longer the planners delay, the more difficult they will find it to cope with the effects of global cooling.
'The Cooling World', *Newsweek,* 28 April 1975

'All respectable scientists know that global cooling is inevitable'
Iben Browning, *Climate Change in the Affairs of Man,* 1975

World tin reserves will run out in 1985, zinc in 1988, petroleum in 1990, natural gas in 1992.
Club of Rome, *Limits to Growth,* 1972

'The battle to feed all of humanity is over ... In the 1970s and 1980s hundreds of millions of people will starve to death in spite of any crash programs embarked upon now. ... I have yet to meet anyone familiar with the situation who thinks that India will be self-sufficient in food by 1971.'
Paul R Ehrlich, *New Scientist,* December 1967

'Thirty four million people could be infected by 1997'.
Government scientist Robert Lacey on the spread of Mad Cow Disease among the human population, *One World,* April 1996

'Barring a miracle' Botswana, Swaziland, Zambia and Zimbabwe will lose one fifth or more of their adult populations within the next decade'
Lester Brown, *The State of the World,* 1999

2. THE CONTEMPORARY RETREAT FROM PRODUCTION

Three unique features make capitalism stand out from earlier systems of class rule. First, only the market system had an intrinsic interest in developing production (to save labour costs). That made them dynamic. Second, only the capitalists recognised the rights of the working class as free agents, by entering into contracts of employment. Third, only the capitalists felt obliged to disguise the origins of their wealth. All other social systems were happy that they wrung their living from the subject class of peasants, serfs or slaves. The capitalists, on the other hand, were forced to disguise they made a living out of the hard work of other people.

They told stories about themselves that cast them as the hardworking, thrifty ones who built up the company (while the workers themselves were generally cast as too lazy to get on).

And though the factory was the place that their profits were made, the capitalists always recoiled from it. They shunned the districts that their workers lived in, and moved their grand houses out into the countryside. As soon as they could afford, they put the day-to-day running of the business into the hands of foremen.

Business was hard. You had to drive reluctant employees to do more work, or force them to accept changes that were not always best for them. There was always some problem on the horizon, with raw materials, markets or rivals.

The capitalist fantasy was always to get out of industry altogether. Their ideal was money that begat more money – without any embarrassing interlude in the mill.

The first industrial nation – Britain – was also the first to try to get out of industry. John Hobson pointed out that between 1890 and 1910 British capitalists were investing their capital abroad, turning themselves into rentiers living off coolie labour in the plantations and mines of the Empire. Industry in Britain was going into liquidation as investors pulled out. It was a trend that could never be seen through to its conclusion – Britain's decadent empire came under pressure from military rivals forcing a return to domestic industrialisation. But still it told us a lot about the capitalists' ambition to retreat from production.

The tendency to retreat from production re-emerged in the 1970s. For investors, industry was an unhappy place. Profit margins were slim. Bloated industries were gripped by inertia. Employees were militant.

Once again, investments went overseas – it seemed easier to lend your money to someone else's business than start up your own. Investment rates fell across the western world. And it was Britain that led the way. Today, according to investment analyst Alan Smithers, Britain's earnings from financial trading far outstrip those from manufacturing.

Corporate raiders like Slater-Walker and James Goldsmith in Britain, and Carl Icahn in America made more money breaking up companies, raiding their pension funds and selling off their assets than they would have by working them. They called it unlocking the shareholder value. The illusion that money begat money, while industry was a just a drag, grew stronger.

The growing complexity of the financial markets showed a strange inventiveness on the part of the capitalists. Money-lending is older than industry, but the ways that investors have created to make money out of money are extraordinary. You have to speculate to accumulate, but too often speculation has become an alternative to investment.

Big industries like Fords, British Gas and British Rail discovered that their assets were worth more than their core business. Fords' investment arm made more on the stock exchange than its car manufacturing. British Gas saw its South American natural gas reserves climb in value while its domestic supply business was a drag. The chairman of the newly privatised British Rail complained that he could make the business very profitable through the sale of its land-holdings if only he did not have to manage railways. In the United States the energy company Enron discovered that it could make more money manipulating financial markets than generating electricity – until it got so greedy that even George Bush's government had to act.

We have seen speculative bubbles in the emerging markets (1998), new technologies (2000) housing (2007) fine art (current). Investments ramp up prices until they spiral. New technology analysts told investors to ignore the price/earning ratio – the relationship between share prices of IT companies and their potential to make money. They reckoned that if the price of the asset continued to rise, then you would make money whether the company ever made anything anyone wants or not. Making money gets divorced from making goods.

The origin of the profits in the production process was so thoroughly disguised that even the investors themselves believed that something could come of nothing, while industry was just a waste of time and effort.

Economic theory reinforced those prejudices when it declared the birth of a New Economy. 'The critical factors of production of this new economy', argued Department of Trade and Industry advisor Charles Leadbeater, 'are not oil, raw materials, armies of cheap labour or physical plant and equipment.' Instead, it was knowledge that created wealth. Citing the latest dot.com IPO Leadbeater fantasised we are 'all in the thin air business'.[8] In America, Clinton's Labour Secretary Robert Reich imagined that the real drivers of wealth would be 'symbolic analysts', people who worked with their minds, from stockbrokers and analysts to hedge-fund managers and pop-stars.

The role industry played in generating wealth was minimised as much as possible. Virtual companies restricted themselves to lean production, or just-in-time production. Manufacturing would be outsourced if possible. The real source of wealth, people imagined, was in the Brand, not the goods. George Gilder of the Financial News Network promised that 'the powers of the mind are everywhere ascendant over the brute force of things', nothing less than the dematerialisation of production was in the offing.[9]

The belief that we had entered a 'post-industrial' age was reinforced in the developed west by the migration of workers from

---

[8] Charles Leadbeater, *Living on Thin Air*, London, Penguin, 2000, p. 14, 18
[9] George Gilder, *Microcosm: the quantum revolution in economics and technology*, New York, Simon and Schuster, 1990

manufacturing into services.[10] Many more people were employed attending to people than making things. Often this change is just a change of employers, not functions. For example, cleaners, or security guards, or designers that were once employed in-house are now bought in from agencies. But in other respects the shift to services represents a transformation of work. For example, early-years childcare, domestic cleaning and catering have all grown – as women do less unpaid work around the house.

The surprising thing about the shift to services is that it has led to an expansion of the workforce. The shift to services is closely linked to lower pay rises, as service sector jobs are less well rewarded – a trend that is masked by the cheapening of consumer goods, so that less cash secures more stuff.[11] Most pointedly, the shift to services in developed countries has tended to flatten the long-term trend towards increased labour productivity, as workers have moved out of capital intensive manufacturing, to labour intensive services.[12] As we shall see, the whole outlook on productivity has changed.

Industry itself did its best to earn the disdain investors felt. In 2002 Mary O'Mahoney of the National Institute for Economic Research found that it was poor leadership and low rates of investment that held back Britain's economic performance.[13] Four years later Dr John Philpot of the Chartered Institute of Personnel and Development found the same thing, writing that 'the vast majority of UK organisations still

---

[10] The Association of Consultant Engineers tells us that there is a 20,000 shortfall in qualified engineers in the UK, Jonathan Glancey, 'Extinction of the engineers', *Guardian,* 15 October, 2007

[11] Economist Doug Henwood estimates that the gains from productivity increases have fallen mostly or wholly to employers over the last thirty years in the US (Doug Henwood, *After the New Economy,* New York, New Press, 2005) – which might understate the gains in the quality of goods (see. Brad DeLong, above).

[12] The country's 'strong labour market performance may', in the words of the DTI, 'actually have ... the effect of lowering average measured productivity', *UK Productivity and competitiveness indicators,* DTI Paper no 9, 2003, p25

[13] Britain's relative productivity performance, March 2002, and see 'Laziness starts at the Top', *Guardian* 2 June 2003

don't make a good enough fist of managing the productive resources they do have, especially their people'.[14]

Entrepreneurs shrunk from industry, but had to find new ways to make money. All of their efforts were put to finding new sources of revenue. Financial speculation was one avenue. Others among their class were adepts at seeking out the government tit.

When the public asked why the billions spent on British schools and the National Health Service did so little good, they only dimly understood that most of the cash had been drawn off to an army of consultants and advisors. But these consultants were not medical consultants or educational advisors. They were business consultants, risk assessors, contractors and recruiters.

Under the expansion of hospitals and schools, most of the money was disbursed as public-private finance initiatives (PFI). Under these make-work schemes shell companies contract others to re-build schools and hospitals. These shell companies demand contracts that put all the burden of risk onto the government, while laying claim to future revenues.

This was the same parasitical cohort that, having worked to get 'New Labour' elected, shifted en masse from the party's HQ in Millbank to the New Millennium Experience Company in 1998. That was their payback, then, and today they and their kind are exacting a monstrous tribute from the London Olympics and Crossrail.

In the case of the 'privatised' National Rail the dependence on government was so great that it was in the end nationalised by mistake, going into receivership. Having squandered the already-subsidized assets, investors demanded compensation.

The booming business consultancy business is not just parasitic upon government, but on other businesses, too. Large corporations that are gripped by indecision can outsource their decision-making. 'Brand strategists' position companies into the future – which is to say the consultants package up the companies' anxieties and sell that package

---

[14] Management misses its chance to reduce the productivity gap, *Guardian*, 20 February 2006

back to the companies as solutions. Nowadays, even designers are more often found redesigning business models than door handles.
Elsewhere, the growing army of litigators chase intellectual property claims against Asian manufacturers they charge with 'ripping off' western designs.

In 1776, the framers of the US constitution thought about copyright and settled on 14 years as a fair period for an inventor to reap the reward of innovation. In the UK today, copyright runs for seventy years *after death*. Big corporations like Disney are leaning on Congress to give them greater extensions. Instead of innovating, companies are using intellectual property lawyers to enforce legal titles to other people's hard work. 'The dynamism of our cultural life depends on taking one another's ideas and building on them', says technology writer John Naughton, 'but we have evolved a legal regime that ... seeks to give to existing right-holders the power to control other people's creativity'.[15]

Even the Gradgrind capitalism of Dickens' day could claim to be laying the grounding for a better future. But today's entrepreneurs have given up on industry. Instead of making money by making things, they do what economists call 'rent-seeking', grubbing around hunting out future revenues streams to divert from other peoples hard work.[16]

There is of course an irony to the way that business schools have taken hold of the post-industrial economic model. And that is that – worldwide – industry has massively expanded (even as it has diminished as a share of work in the developed world). The expansion of market economies into the former socialist and developing world has created thousands of new cities, factories and industrial centres.

---

[15] John Naughton, 'The very model of a modern creative society?' *Observer*, 25 March 2007

[16] Michael Perelman's argument that capitalism survives by 'primitive accumulation' might be overstated but he is definitely pointing to an important new trend that I wrongly dismissed before. See his books *The Invention of Capitalism,* Durham, Duke University Press, 2000 and *Steal this Idea,* New York, Palgrave Macmillan, 2002, and see Christian Zeller, 'From the Gene to the Globe', *Review of International Political Economy* 15:1 February 2008: 86–115

Pointedly, though, these have tended to be expansion of the factory system on the basis of the existing level of technology. Capital is growing extensively, by incorporating more employees, rather than intensively, replacing workers by better technique. So even in the Far East, the new factories are not that different from the 'job-rich' growth that we see in the West. Still, China's and India's growth is the focal point of a lot of anti-industrial hostilities.

The hyper-modern world of the old New Economy seems a million miles from environmental thinking. But it does have one thing in common – a loathing for the very industry that lays the basis of our latter-day well-being. In the end the gurus of the New Economy lacked the moral standing to justify their climbing incomes. There was more than a little relief when the dot.com boom crashed. The whole 'irrational exuberance' was difficult to stomach. Even Charles Leadbeater had to concede that we cannot live on thin air. But the underlying hatred for industry was about to find a more winning moral framework, environmentalism.

3. GREEN CAPITALISTS

Today's business leaders do not tuck their shirts in. They listen to Tom Peters and Charles Handy and follow Bill Gates and Steve Jobs. Every winter the cream of them get together in Davos Switzerland. Bill Clinton goes there, and so does Al Gore. They meet celebrities like Bono and Angelina Jolie, or listen to financier and philanthropist George Soros or the Bank of England economist Nicholas Stern talking about the environment. The business elite has been meeting at Davos since the First World War. The Alpine Ski resort started the jet-setting exclusivity that has been the model for international forums ever since. In Olympian detachment the wealthy look down on the *hoi polloi* in the knowledge that they could not afford the airfare. In 2007 'more than 2,000 of the world's elite travelled by plane, helicopter and chauffeured car to attend meetings in Switzerland where they waxed lyrical about the need to curb greenhouse gas emissions,' and produced 8,264 tons of greenhouse gases.[17]

Some of the world's wealthiest people are also its greenest. More and more of them make their money being green – they are the pioneers of Green Capitalism.

Al Gore's 10,000-square-foot, 20-room, eight-bathroom home in Nashville (he owns two others) burns up more electricity each month than most American families do in a year. Since telling us that we need to consume less in the surprise-hit film *An Inconvenient Truth* Gore's energy burn has increased from an average of 16,200 kilowatt-hours per month in 2005, to 18,400 per month in 2006.[18] While he was Vice-

---

[17] Reuters, 27 January 2007; http://www.davosclimatealliance.org/footprint/footprint_2007.php
[18] 'Gore's home uses more than 20 times the national average', Press Release, Tennessee Centre for Policy Research, 26 February 2007, http://www.tennesseepolicy.org/main/article.php?article_id=367

President, US energy consumption grew by about five quadrillion Btu, but production slumped.[19]

Gore has been knocked for his use of private jets electioneering and promoting his film, but says that he buys carbon credits to offset his energy consumption. In fact Paramount Pictures buy carbon credits on his behalf – from a company he chairs and part-owns, Generation Investment Management.[20] Gore's wealth was inherited from his father Albert Gore, a US Congressman and tobacco farmer. Since failing to become President in 2000, Gore hawked political influence to big business and is on the board of Apple Computers (where he has stock worth $6 million), an advisor to Google (with stock of $30 million) a chairman of cable news channel Current TV and charges $175,000 to lecture: his current wealth is more than $100 million.[21]

In 1997, the corporate raider Sir James Goldsmith flew in his private jet, while dying, from Spain to France to save his heirs from inheritance tax. **Zac Goldsmith,** b. 1975, inherited £300 million from his father. After working for an NGO in the Himalayas, Eton-educated Zac bought *The Ecologist* magazine his uncle Edward founded in 1970 and used it to lead the campaign against the biotech company Monsanto. The organic farm on his Tavistock estate in Devon is Goldsmith's hobby; his real investments are spread across the gaming industry. The Tory candidate for Richmond lives the high life, but does not believe that everyone should: 'the earth cannot sustain the process of third world countries catching up with us'.[22] 'It is good to be part of the solution, not part of the problem' says Sheherazade Goldsmith, promoting her organic groceries. But if the millionaire Sheherazade Goldsmith is part of the solution, then maybe it is the wrong problem.

---

[19] Energy Information Administration, Total Energy, Energy in the United States: 1635-2000, Figure 3, http://www.eia.doe.gov/emeu/aer/eh/frame.html
[20] *USA Today,* 10 August 2006
[21] *Fast Company Magazine,* July 2007, http://www.fastcompany.com/magazine/117/features-gore.html; and see Steven Swinford, 'A convenient £50m for green guru Gore', *Sunday Times,* 9 December 2007 , 'Gore draws Silicon Valley into climate-change battle', *Financial Times,* 13 November 2007
[22] *Guardian,* 7 November 2002

Anita Roddick, 1942-2007, sold her global franchise of 1407 Body Shops to French cosmetics giant L'Oreal for £256 million the previous year. Since 1976 the Body Shop sold itself as a protest against that inhumane Thatcherism. But in fact Roddick developed a new style of Green Capitalism that is learning to make profits without growth. What Roddick sold was ideas more than goods. The Fair Trade element of the Body Shop's business was always small – a loss leader to interest customers who would leave with a small over-priced pot of avocado cream. Critics alleged that the Mexican Indian natives used to illustrate the Body Shop's American Express Campaign were exploited; or that local producers in the Solomon Islands and the Brazilian Kayapo Indians were left in the lurch; in 1996 the Body Shop pulled the plug on a deal to buy shea butter from a town in Ghana, leaving the local economy, having all geared up to meet the order, in tatters. Anita had the idea of employing the Nepalese making writing paper. As you can imagine the production process was pretty primitive, but the villagers leaped on any suggestion of assistance and set to the writing paper venture with gusto. The writing paper had big lumps in it and frayed at the edges. Roddick was right that that was no great problem as it just lent the product some handwoven authenticity. Where she miscalculated was in estimating the market. Body Shop customers were just too self-centred to ever write to anyone, and the paper was a poor competitor to lilac eye cream. Great bales of wrinkly Nepalese paper went unsold. The low productivity of the venture meant that it was too expensive to sell through any other outlet. After a couple of years the Body Shop left the village, as mysteriously as they came, leaving a score of unemployed and under-skilled paper makers.

Jeremy Leggett, b. 1957c. His Solar Century business is the fastest growing alternative energy company. It turns over £4.2 million a year, and just invested £13.5m – which is not entirely surprising since the government is currently committed to paying for one half of the cost of installing its solar panels.[23] 'Clients' are mostly government subsidies from Transport for London, The Environment Agency, the National Trust, the Crown Estates and the BBC, or they are guilty greenwashers like Tesco, GlaxoSmithKline, Barratt Homes, Sainsbury's and Texaco. Leggett, who sits on the government's renewable energy panel, is a former oil industry consultant who worked for Greenpeace before launching his solar panel business with £7 million. Solar Century launders its profits through a 'charity' Solar Aid, whose patron is Cate Blanchett, and Leggett chairs, disbursing grants to Africans to buy Solar Century panels and gadgets. Solar Aid's website encourages donations to 'offset your emissions', which you can calculate on a handy pull-down menu.

Peter Mond, b. 1948, the fourth Baron Melchett, is heir to the Imperial Chemicals Industry fortune heaped up by his grandfather Alfred Mond (from the hard labours of people like my grandfather, ICI electrician, John Paterson). A youthful minister in James Callaghan's Labour government, Eton and Cambridge educated Melchett turned his back on politics to run first the Rambler's Association, then Greenpeace and now the organic farmer's lobby, the Soil Association. Melchett owns an 890-acre farm himself but was still arrested for tearing down genetically modified crops planted as part of government tests. Melchett shocked his fellow activists, though, when he accepted a job with the PR company tasked with promoting GM, Burson Marsteller – a portfolio he has expanded to take on work with Ikea, Asda and Wal-Mart; Melchett also sits on government, BBC and European Union committees, and charges up to £2500 to speak.

As well as the big green swinging dicks, there are plenty of lesser opportunists making a living out of retailing the environmental cause. Restauranteurs-turned-television producers **Jamie Oliver** (b. 1975), owner of Fresh One Productions, and **Hugh Fearnley-Whittingstall** (b. 1965) have both milked the formula of green activism: Oliver with his

---

[23] Leggett even had the nerve to complain when the grants were held up while government officials investigated whether supported schemes were really taking going ahead, 'Green firms attack DTI over grant fiasco', *Guardian,* 20 April 2007

Jamie's School Dinners programme for Channel 4, that combined a school catering makeover (and a lot of unpaid overtime for cooks) with a lobby of the Education Department, but only led to a reduction in take-up; following the success of his River Cottage TV show and cookbook, Eton and Oxford educated Fearnley-Whittingstall is investing in a local-produce competitor in Axminster – while persuading Channel 4 to fund his campaign to stop Tesco opening there.

In the twentieth century, armaments manufacturers held a privileged place among industrialists. Because their output was the means of national defence, they had a special call on governments. The industry was tightly inter-woven into officialdom – a relationship that President Eisenhower highlighted when he warned against growth of the Military-Industrial Complex.[24] Daddy Warbucks loomed large in American life, as he did in Li'l Orphan Annie's. Munitions firms effectively blackmailed governments to buy their goods, out of fear of annihilation at the hands of their enemies in the arms race. Today the green capitalists strong-arm local and national governments, householders and other industries into buying their products out of fear of climate catastrophe. Back then people began to suspect that the arms makers were inventing threats to sell guns. Today, the same people that are talking up the threat of climate change are selling us the solar panels and carbon offsets.

The 'Greenwashers'

Alongside these green entrepreneurs, some traditional businesses have remodelled themselves Green. Today, even Rupert Murdoch's **Sky Broadcasting** is a 'carbon neutral company' – how easy it is to shuck off the record of union-busting and dumbing-down, just by planting some trees (or buying indulgences from Pope Gore, or Father Leggett).

L'Oreal, the Paris-based multi-national that Anita Roddick criticised for animal-testing its products bought out the Body Shop franchise – keeping Roddick on as an advisor.

---

[24] In David Mermelstein (ed), *Economics,* Random House, New York, 1973, p. 178

Anglo-Dutch giant **Unilever** bought out Ben & Jerry's ethically aware ice cream business in 2000 and kept on Cohen and Greenfield as 'goodwill ambassadors';[25] Unilever-owned Ben & Jerry's started up the Climate Change College, to educate young people about global warming in 2005.

Tesco Chief Executive Sir Terry Leahy has pledged £25 million for a 'sustainable consumption institute' at Manchester University, part of a programme to train consumers to 'accept price increases' necessary for greener lifestyles.[26]

Not to be outdone the US retail giant **Wal-Mart** is to use its buying power to squeeze suppliers to reduce transport and packaging costs, so that 'customers could do the right thing for this planet' ... and for Wal-Mart.[27]

Businesses outside of the manufacturing sector do a lot better in the green audit because they emit less carbon. The Geneva-based company Covalence tracks the ethical reputation of multinationals. In a reversal of the long-standing prejudice against usury, banks come out as second most ethical of all businesses. **HSBC, Barclays, Royal Bank of Scotland** and **Lloyds TSB** all got top marks in the ethical audit because – lo and behold! – they are kinder to the environment than businesses that make things. Of course Lloyds can promise to reduce its carbon footprint by 30 per cent by 2012 because it does not have that big a carbon footprint in the first place. Still, the ethics of protecting the environment are bound to favour finance over manufacturing. Lucky for finance-heavy British capitalists, but not necessarily for consumers.

One reason that companies are getting greener is that they have been asked to. In the year 2000, then Prime Minister Tony Blair asked businesses to draw up an environmental audit over the next year. Activists pour scorn on business for 'Greenwashing'. But since they are the ones pressuring business to respond to the green agenda, it seems mean to tell them off when they do it. No doubt there was a lot of

---

[25] *Boston Phoenix*, 8 August 2003, http://72.166.46.24//boston/news_features/qa/documents/03073228.asp
[26] Guardian, 13 September 2007
[27] 'Wal Mart boss says he will press suppliers in race to go green', *Guardian*, 3 February 2007, http://www.guardian.co.uk/frontpage/story/0,,2004451,00.html

cynicism in the initial attempts to paint businesses greener, but over time, Chief Executives got to think like environmentalists. Why would they not? Green business was a success.

The Birth of Green Capitalism

Environmental campaigners object to the 'greenwashing' of corporations. 'Greenwashing' means big polluters trying to paint themselves green. The idea is that the pressure from radicals has forced the businesses to pretend to be green, to cover up the harm they do to the environment. Something like that does happen, but it is by no means the whole picture.

The usual account of greenwashing gets things back to front. The growth of environmentalism is not a case of radicals influencing big business. It is a case of big business influencing radicals.

Greens do not know their own history. The modern environmental movement was launched by big business (only turning 'anti-capitalist' later – and that was just a pose to wring a better deal from the suits).

Just to get this straight, we are not talking here about the old conservation movement. That has been about for centuries. Romantic Conservatives like John Ruskin, Thomas Carlyle, Martin Heidegger and Lady Eva Balfour all made reactionary protests against the modern world.

The modern environmental movement began around thirty-five years ago. The elite industrialists of the Club of Rome, led by Fiat's Aurelio Peccei, and British government scientist Alexander King commissioned the report *The Limits to Growth*. It was drawn up by MIT computer scientists Jay Forrester and Donella and Dennis Meadows who predicted economic collapse by resource depletion by 2100. In Britain, millionaire Edward Goldsmith launched the *Ecologist* in 1970, while the government launched a Save It campaign to cut energy use (and undermine the bargaining power of the National Union of Miners).

The background to this elite environmentalism was a fierce campaign by business to restore profits by cutting wages. By 'greenwashing' this campaign against working-class living standards as saving the environment, the business elite were trying to disguise their own pecuniary motives. Trade Union leaders must support 'cuts in consumption' wrote Margaret Laws Smith for the Conservation Society. The Worldwatch Institute's Lester Brown demanded 'labor union leaders exercise restraint'.[28]

The environmentalists were not just exercised about rising working class living standards. They resented the very existence of the masses. Population control was one of their big campaigns. Richard Nixon's US National State Security Memorandum 200 called for 'constructive actions to lower fertility'[29]

Cutting working class living standards is still at the core of environmentalism today. 'I hope that the recession being forecast by some economists materialises', writes George Monbiot in 2007. 'I recognise that recession causes hardship' he explains, and 'that it would cause some people to lose their jobs and homes.'[30]

Back in the 1970s and 80s radicals knew that the environmentalists were the enemy. Marxist Istvan Meszaros accused the capitalists of hiding under 'the umbrella of universal "ecological concern"'. And all of this with the 'additional bonus of making people at large pay, under the pretext of "human survival", for the survival of a social economic system', namely capitalism.[31] In the *International Socialist Journal* Mike Simons wrote: 'the key idea of the new environmental movement, "that the earth cannot cope with the strains inflicted upon it", is one of the oldest reactionary arguments around'.[32]

---

[28] Margaret Laws Smith, *Towards the Creation of a Sustainable Economy,* London, Conservation Society, 1975, p, 9; Lester Brown, *Building a Sustainable Community,* New York, Worldwatch Institute, 1981, p. 122

[29] Stephen Mumford, *The Life and Death of NSSM 200,* N Carolina, Centre for Research on Population and Security, 1996, p 499

[30] George Monbiot, 'In this age of diamond saucepans, only a recession makes sense', *Guardian,* 9 October 2007

[31] Istvan Meszaros, *The Necessity of Social Control,* London, Merlin, 1971, p. 19

[32] Mike Simons, 'Red and Green – socialists and the ecology movement', *International Socialist Journal,* London, Winter 1988, No, 37, p. 53. Later on the International Socialists made their peace with the environmentalists, embracing the anti-globalisation protests in Seattle in 1999.

Certainly, the key activists of the environmental movement were remarkably well-heeled. Apart from the Etonians Zac Goldsmith and Lord Peter Melchett already described there is; the Green Party's Jonathan Porritt (Eton and Oxford) heir to the Baronet Porritt; Tory Chairman's son George Monbiot (Stowe and Oxford); Mark Brown (Radley School), heir to the Vestey fortune, who was acquitted of leading the Carnival Against Capitalism of June 1999. Charles Secrett (Cranleigh), executive director of Friends of the Earth, explains the toff-appeal of environmentalism: 'Among the aristocrats there is a sense of noblesse oblige . . . feeling of stewardship towards the land'.[33]

Two big changes made the green movement mainstream. The first was that the left lost its way when the Soviet Union fell apart. Already battered by years of right-wing governments, the left saw the failure of the USSR as proof that socialist ideology was finished. The traditional left's nadir, 1989, was a turning point for green parties who won eight per cent of the vote in Europe.[34] Disoriented radicals flocked to support the green parties they once dismissed – hoping to make an environmentalist case against capitalism.

But even picking up the left-wing protest vote would not have made environmentalism as influential as it is today. The second change that made green mainstream was, as already described, the capitalist retreat from production. Though they won the Cold War, business leaders were in no mood to party. On the contrary, without a battle plan against the socialists to keep them focussed, their worries about growth only got worse.

The capitalist class were already recoiling in distaste at the dirty business of making stuff. Here was a movement that made sense of their own bad feelings. Some older business leaders, often in dirtier industries, tried to face the protestors down. But many more were already half way convinced that the environmentalists had a point. They listened to what the greens had to say – giving them more importance sometimes than they deserved. As one critic explained: 'The doubts that beset international elites are the soil that nurtures the anti-capitalist

---

[33] *Guardian,* 5 May 2000
[34] Phil Macnaghten and John Urry, *Contested Natures,* London, Sage, 1998, p. 79

movement, which re-presents those inner worries in an external and oppositional form.'[35]

Some greenwashing was, at first, just public relations. But the MDs were not immune from the green mood sweeping the rest of society. In 2002, McDonald's, Rio Tinto, Nike, Nestlé, and British American Tobacco all produced 'sustainability reviews'.[36]

As an oil company Anglo-Dutch Shell was in the firing line. In the company brochure *There is no Alternative,* Shell makes 'a commitment to contribute to sustainable development' and 'achieving a more sustainable world'.[37]

British Petroleum was mocked for its slogan 'Beyond Petroleum' – which they explain as follows 'the development of new ways in which to produce and supply oil and gas – through clean fuels, through greater efficiency and through substitution – particularly of gas for coal in the power sector'; and eventually 'the development of new fuels which can over a long period begin to provide new choices'.[38]

But taking on board the protestors' moans did not calm the greens – on the contrary, it just made them bolder. On 23 October 2003, 'Rising Tide', a green umbrella group, protested at BP's AGM, heckling Chairman Lord Browne, and passing around a spoof Annual Report. Friends of the Earth, who had been drawn into talks with BP, announced a re-think: 'We are not going to be cosy with them because they are doing bad things'.[39]

In 2004 Shell was in trouble for bigging-up its oil reserves. Shareholders' anger got mixed up with environmental protests. The new chairman Ron Oxburgh signaled his willingness to listen to criticisms by acceding the green case against his industry: 'I am very worried for the planet'. 'Multinationals are not popular but there are

---

[35] Quoted in David Chandler and Gideon Baker, *Constructing Global Civil Society,* London, Palgrave, 2005, p. 86
[36] *Guardian,* 19 August 2002
[37] *There is No Alternative,* London, Shell International Limited, 2002, p. 22
[38] 'Beyond Petroleum', BP http://www.bp.com/sectiongenericarticle.do?categoryId=9010219&contentId=7019491, viewed on 14 December 2007
[39] *Guardian,* 23 October 2003

things that you can't do without them' Oxburgh pleaded.[40] This is how he won back the high ground – making his shareholders all feel a bit bad about what they were supposed to be doing to the planet and making his own mistakes look like small beer.

Green activists rubbish corporate environmentalism as 'greenwashing'. But the truth is that most of the leading green activists – Melchett, Tony Juniper, Jonathan Porritt, Des Wilson, Sara Parkin, the New Economics Foundation – have made a very good living writing Corporate Social Responsibility documents and doing other PR. Greenies get jobs as consultants and trainers, hectoring the unenlightened suits. When green activists frame their criticisms aggressively, that is often just their way of negotiating a better deal.

Just look at who is funding America's environmental critics: **Chevron, Exxon, Philip Morris, Mobil, Morgan Guaranty, Arco, Du Pont, Ciba Geigy, Bank of Boston, Ford Foundation, General Electric, HJ Heinz Co., Monsanto,** *New York Times*, **Proctor and Gamble.**[41] For the British Greens Porritt and Parkin's Forum for the Future took money from **ICI, BP, Tesco and Blue Circle.**[42]

Greens posed as anti-capitalists around the turn of the millennium. They led some performance art rioting outside the Group of Seven, WTO, World Bank, IMF and EU summits in Seattle, Prague, Gothenburg and Nice. Another World is Possible, they said. 'Smash Capitalism!' read their posters. 'I know I've set myself an impossible task, but I'm not going to be happy until there is complete change in the world,' said Zac Goldsmith.[43] Tony Juniper described the way the environmentalists changed their tune: 'For the past 10 years we've been locating ourselves more in the bigger economic debate and less in the 'save the whales' type debate.'[44]

But the Greens have very quickly got used to this world, which has proved so accommodating to their distaste for industry. Smash

---

[40] *Guardian,* 17 June 2004
[41] Ron Arnold and Alan Gottlieb, *Trashing the Economy,* Washington D.C., Merril Press, 1994
[42] George Monbiot, 'Sleeping with the enemy', *Guardian,* 4 September 2001
[43] *Guardian,* 7 November 2002
[44] *Observer,* 14 July 2002

Capitalism? Jonathan Porritt is happier to re-organise it. His latest book is called, *Capitalism: as if the world mattered.* 'These companies are at the forefront of a revolution in business behaviour', said Green Party spokesman turned corporate mouthpiece Des Wilson, defending himself against the charge of 'sleeping with the enemy'.[45] 'It would seem that I was wrong about big business', wrote George Monbiot, 'the obstacle is not the market but the government'.[46] And despite calling for a 'complete change' Zac Goldsmith – since named Tory candidate for Richmond upon Thames – was careful to add that he is not opposed to business.

Just as the environmentalists have learned to love the market again, business has embraced the opportunities offered by the new green thinking. A welter of business books offer new ways to 'Cut Carbon and grow profits',[47] or turn 'Green to Gold'[48] ('how smart companies use environmental strategy to innovate, create value and build a competitive advantage'). Environmental policies are not greenwashing, they are big business.

---

[45] *Guardian,* 16 January 2002
[46] *Guardian,* 20 September 2005
[47] Kenny Tang, Ruth Yeoh, *Cut Carbon, grow profits,* London, Middlesex University Press, 2007
[48] DC Esty, *Green to Gold,* New Haven, Yale University Press, 2006

4. MANUFACTURED SCARCITY: THE PROFITS OF DEINDUSTRIALISATION

> *'Of course companies that sell climate change solutions stand to benefit as greenhouse gas emissions come to bear a price tag.'* Daniel Esty Hillhouse, Professor of Environmental Law, Harvard University, [49]

As we have seen, the corporate raiders of the 1980s first worked out that you might be able to make more money downsizing, or even breaking up industry than building it up. It is a perverse result of the profit motive that private gain should grow out of public decay. But even the corporate raiders never dreamt of making deindustrialisation into an avowed policy goal and make the rest of us pay for it.

What some of the cannier Green Capitalists worked out is that scarcity increases price, and manufacturing scarcity can increase returns. What could be more old hat, they said, than trying to make money by making things cheaper? That was rubbished as a 'race to the bottom'.

Of course there is a point to all this. If labour gets too efficient the chances of wringing more profits from industry get less. The more productive labour is, the lower, in the end, will be the rate of return on investments. That is because the source of new value is living labour; but greater investment in new technologies tends to replace living labour with machines, which produce no additional value of their own.[50] Over time the rate of return must fall. Business theory calls this the diminishing rate of return.[51] Businessmen know it as the 'race for the bottom' – the competitive pressure to make goods cheaper and cheaper, making it that much harder to sell enough to make a profit.

---

[49] The Green List, *Guardian* supplement, p 29, 5 November 2007
[50] See Karl Marx, *Capital,* Volume Three, 'The law of the tendency of the rate of profit to fall', London, Lawrence and Wishart, 1959, pp 211-240
[51] 'The Origin Of The Law Of Diminishing Returns', Edwin Cannan, 1813-15, *Economic Journal,* vol 2, 1892

Super efficient labour would make the capitalistic organisation of industry redundant.

Manufacturing scarcity, restricting output and so driving up prices is one short-term way to secure profits and maybe even the profit-system. Of course that also would also abandoning the historic justification for capitalism, that it increased output and living standards. Environmentalism might turn out to be the way to save capitalism, just at the point when industrial development had shown it to be redundant.

Some of the most destructive examples of manufactured scarcity are carbon trading, 'clean energy', 'Nature Reserve' land retirement and green belt housebuilding restrictions.

Carbon Trading

The United Nations' Kyoto deal on climate change of 1997 laid the legal basis of carbon trading. On the grounds that CO_2 emissions were damaging to the climate, Kyoto called for limits. Under the two schemes that follow on from Kyoto, the European Union Allocation (EUA) and the UN's Clean Development Mechanism legal titles to emit a given amount of CO_2 are distributed to industry. These titles are transferable, creating a market in carbon trading rights.

These titles to emit carbon are not real goods, but monopoly rights created by laws. Once they are traded, though, they act just like commodities.[52] Because they are limited in number, and needed to take part in a lot of industry, they are susceptible to big price swings, and therefore ripe for speculation. Financial markets being what they are, the speculative potential of carbon trading could hardly be ignored. Here was another opportunity to make money for doing nothing. In fact, here was an opportunity to make money by stopping things from being made. Even the most insipid capitalist could not resist.

---

[52] 'Objects that in themselves are no commodities, such as conscience, honour, &c., are capable of being offered for sale by their holders, and of thus acquiring, through their price, the form of commodities.' Karl Marx, *Capital,* Vol. 1, Moscow, Progress, 1974, p 105

The European Union Allocation was overpriced at its initial offering, at €30 a tonne. Within a year, the value of the market in EUAs doubled in value to €205 billion. Unfortunately, 170 million too many were issued. Individual companies, particularly energy companies, soon noticed that they had millions of tonnes of EUAs they did not need, and so they sold their unused carbon licenses on, making huge profits. A 2005 report by IPA Energy Consulting found that the six UK electricity generators stood to earn some £800m in each of the three years of the scheme, by selling their spare EUAs.

A separate report by Open Europe, in July 2006, found that UK oil companies were also poised to make a lot of free money: £10.2m for Esso; £17.9m for BP; and £20.7m for Shell. Beyond Petroleum indeed – why bother refining petroleum when the EU will give you millions in carbon trading titles. It was so much easier for energy companies to by-pass electricity generation, and trade in fictitious legal titles. Who was paying for them? Universities and hospitals in the UK, underallocated EUAs, were buyers. The University of Manchester alone shelled out £92,500 for its carbon rights.[53] Of course, once the big EUA traders had sold them on, the prices collapsed, leaving public utilities holding overvalued EUAs. Hewlett Johnson, the 'Red' Dean of Canterbury, used to say that if the capitalists could put a price tag on the air we breathe they would sell it back to us. Little did he know that fifty years later hospitals and colleges would be paying oil and energy companies for a legal title to a share of the atmosphere.

The creation of a market in carbon emission rights also makes a new role of broker for those rights. With its eye on the prize, the World Bank proposes to broker rights between the developed and developing world. This trade it estimates could earn the Bank $100 million a year.[54] US companies are gearing up for the expected adoption of carbon trading (already a voluntary climate change market in Chicago has seen its titles increase in value five times). Morgan Stanley is investing $3 billion to trade carbon, and a host of new companies, like EcoSecurities

---

[53] Nick Davies, 'The Truth about Kyoto', *Guardian,* 2 June 2007
[54] Sustainable Energy and Economy Network, 'The World Bank and G7', http://www.seen.org/pages/ifis/wbstill/wbgrafx.shtml viewed on 14 October 2007

and Trading Emissions (TRE) are setting up shop in New York.[55] The Oxford-based EcoSecurities expects to trade £38 million in 2007 and make £6 million, but trade £96 million and make £52 million in 2008.[56] If the roller-coaster of EUA prices is anything to go by, brokers' ambitions are realistic.

It is important to remember that Carbon Trading generates income from limits on output – and carbon emissions are a cipher for industrial output generally, since most industry is also carbon production. For individual businesses it might seem to make little sense to see output limited. But for larger businesses it can be advantageous for the bar of entry to your sector to be raised higher, so restricting competition. And creating monopoly conditions, businesses can pass on the additional costs to their customers. The desire to raise the bar of entry is behind the European Union's preference for the Kyoto summit agreement, and China's opposition. Carbon limits favour mature industrial nations against their developing rivals.

Alongside the official business-to-business trade in carbon licenses, there is a voluntary trade in carbon offsetting. The carbon-offset business is worth $34 billion and expected to double in size by 2010[57] – even though its products are about as useful for the environment as cryogenic suspension is for longevity. Whereas carbon trading deals in UN or EU licenses to emit, carbon offsetting still operates for now in a voluntary framework. Such, however, is the moral pressure that offsetting will become obligatory in more and more places. The House of Commons Environmental Audit Committee has leant hard on airlines to include offsetting schemes in their pricing.[58] Warren Buffet's private jet company NetJets has made offsetting mandatory for all customers adding £2720 to its prices.

We have already met some carbon-offsetting cowboys in SolarCentury/SolarAid MD Jeremy Leggett and Al Gore. Elsewhere disquiet about the industry is widespread. HSBC looked at offsetting

---

[55] *New York Times,* 28 December 2006
[56] 'How to profit from Carbon Trading', *MoneyWeek,* 27 October 2006
[57] *Financial Times* 25 April 2007
[58] House of Commons Environmental Audit Committee, 'The Voluntary Carbon Offset Market', Sixth Report of Session 2006-7, London, HMSO, 23 July 2007

only to draw the conclusion that 'the police, the fraud squad and trading standards need to be looking into this'. Offsetting companies themselves agree that 'there are credibility issues and there are cowboys around'.[59] EasyJet spokesman Toby Nicol objected that 'between 25 per cent and 30 per cent of every pound put in by consumers would go into administrating [sic] the company'.[60]

What is offsetting? Where it is not just pocketing gullible people's money, it is mostly planting trees, usually in the developing world. In practice that means taking land out of production that would otherwise be farmed for food. Manufacturing scarcity is big business.

Clean Energy and Negawatts

In 1997 the Club of Rome collaborated with Amory Lovins of the Rocky Mountain Institute to launch a new report *Factor Four* that promised to 'halve resource use' while doubling wealth. The message was that you could get rich saving the planet. A privileged few did indeed double their wealth; but for the rest it was just a case of halving resources.

Immodestly, Lovins made his own California energy scheme the main example of savings in *Factor Four*. His well-paid advice to the state of California was that it was a big mistake to adopt a system that rewarded increased electricity output with increased profits. Such a system would naturally tend to boost output. Instead rewards for cutting energy use were needed. Rather than getting paid for additional *megawatts* the utility companies should be rewarded for saving power use: *negawatts*.

The impact on energy generation was decisive. 'Around 1980, Pacific Gas and Electricity Company was planning to build some 10-20 power stations' according to Lovins.

---

[59] Jonathan Shopley chief executive of CarbonNeutral Company, Francis Sullivan for HSBC, *Guardian*, 18 June 2007
[60] *Guardian* 23 July 2007

But by 1992, PG&E was planning to build no more power stations, and in 1993, it permanently dissolved its engineering and construction division. Instead as its 1992 Annual Report pronounced, it planned to get at least three quarters of its new power needs in the 1990s from more efficient use by its customers.[61]

Of course the PG&E was not getting three quarters of its new power needs from anywhere: it had just reduced its output. But manufacturing energy scarcity did indeed grow somebody's cash wealth: Enron's. With these artificial caps on energy production the generating companies could start to hike up the charges to utility companies, including PG&E, now unable to meet its own customers' demands. Those energy companies were owned by Enron.

ENRON: ENVIRONMENTAL CHAMPION

'**One US energy giant, Enron, has emerged as the world leader in renewable energy investment,' said Climate Institute President John Topping** 'Enron has significantly lowered the cost of renewable energy, and triggered energy industry investment in both solar and wind power. Ken Lay has spearheaded this effort by Enron."

In 2001 Enron led corporations in the Pew Centre on Global Climate Change lobbying for the US to sign the Kyoto agreement.

EPA Climate Protection Award, 1998
Enron received this award in recognition of its "exemplary efforts and achievements in protecting the global climate." Enron was one of 19 individuals and organizations chosen from an international field and judged by an international panel selected from industry, government and international non-governmental organizations.

---

[61] Amory Lovins, L Hunter Lovins and Ernst von Wiezsacker, *Factor Four: Doubling wealth, halving resource use,* London, Earthscan, p. 160

Chief Executive Kenneth Lay turned Enron from a company that made its money generating power into one that made its money trading finance. Whatever else it was doing, there was no denying that Enron was cutting back its own CO_2 emissions and getting rich doing it. One company memo stated that the Kyoto treaty 'would do more to promote Enron's business than will almost any other regulatory initiative'.[62]

Amory Lovins' negawatt revolution in California was Enron's wet dream. Having shut down its own generation capacity, PG&E was at the mercy of Enron's market manipulation. Buying surplus electricity on the open market PG&E was royally fleeced, losing $12 billion. Utility bills rose by *nine times*. Enron took advantage of the restricted market and cut electricity to California. They even invented reasons to take power plants offline while California was blacked out. Enron official joked that they were stealing one million dollars a day from California.[63] The PG&E that Lovins held up as a model went bankrupt and had to be bailed out by the state of California.

The negawatt revolution in California was supposed to reward savings and alternative energy generation. In the event manufacturing scarcity only rewarded Enron's crooked speculators, while penalising consumers.

Sadly, the lessons of the 'negawatt revolution' have been buried in the outrage about Enron's fraudulent market manipulation. Few people noticed that Enron's executives were taking advantage of an artificial scarcity in energy supply engineered by Amory Lovins and the PG&E all the time in close association with Enron's favourite green lobby, the National Resources Defence Council.[64]

Few of Enron's critics noticed that it was the very model of an environmentally friendly, post-industrial company and one that had

---

[62] How Environmentalists Sold Out to Help Enron, *PR Watch Newsletter,* Third Quarter 2003, Volume 10, No. 3

[63] 'Tapes Show Enron Arranged Plant Shutdown' *The New York Times* 04 February 2005

[64] How Environmentalists Sold Out to Help Enron, *PR Watch Newsletter,* Third Quarter 2003, Volume 10, No. 3

taken Amory Lovins' goal of doubling wealth by halving resource use to heart.

Saving energy is of course good sense – as long as that is done by resource efficiency. The Club of Rome's claim that manipulating market prices to create incentives for reducing energy output can create efficiency is confused. All that achieved was an artificial shortage – the condition for ramping up utility bills. The market incentive for energy efficiency comes with reduced bills from savings in raw materials and generation. Normal prices would give customers the incentive to reduce their electricity consumption in turn.

But amazingly the Enron-Lovins model of restricting supply is the one that is being adopted around the world. Utility companies are rewarding consumers for reducing their consumption from central power stations and encouraging domestic-sited energy generation, through windmills and solar panels. Playing on Californians' distrust of the power companies the Environmental Protection Agency is planning to add solar power to one million new homes – paid for by another surcharge on utility bills.[65] In Britain, the government is introducing regulations to make all new homes carbon-neutral. The current goal of carbon-neutral homes reverses the division of labour that saw specialised energy producers distribute electricity, turning it into an eighteenth-century cottage industry. The simple economic lesson that mass production avoids reproduction of effort has been lost. Nothing could be more wasteful, or more guaranteed to create new scarcity.

Land retirement creates food scarcity

In the Democratic Republic of the Congo, Sankuru villagers turned to hunting okapi and monkeys for food after an epidemic wiped out most of their pigs. Now they are forbidden to because their land has been declared a gigantic nature reserve – 11,803 square miles (bigger than the state of Massachusetts), which pushes the share of the DRC that is protected from eight per cent to ten. The reserve is supposed to protect

---

[65] *Guardian*, 6 August 2004

the bonobo chimpanzees and okapi, as well as limiting climate change. The Sankuru villagers are now the target of public awareness campaigns and park rangers to stop them feeding on the wildlife. Campaigners accuse them of believing that monkey meat increases potency, demonising the diet that necessity forced on them. The Bonobo Conservation Initiative say that the Chimpanzees are our closest relative – though it is not clear they would extend the same courtesy to the people of Sankuru. Indeed, the Initiative thinks that the bonobos are a step up from recent Congolese history:

> Bonobos exemplify how society can be successfully organized through cooperation and sharing of resources, as opposed to competition, territoriality and violence (as demonstrated by our other closest primate relatives, the male-dominated chimpanzees). Further, bonobos show how love – and love-making – can ease tensions and keep the peace.[66]

The bonobos seem to make Sankuru special, but the truth is that setting land aside from exploitation is something that is happening more and more, all over the world. In Gabon, President Omar Bongo created a nature reserve of 1.4 million acres to stop logging and elephant hunting in the Minkebe Forest, part of a 10,000 square mile network of protected areas throughout central Africa.[67] From 2002 more than 122 million acres of rain forest are protected under the Amazon Region Protected Areas – a scheme sponsored by the World Bank, the World Wildlife Fund, the German Development Bank and the Brazilian Government.[68]

In the US, the Federal Land Policy and Management Act of 1976 increased the preserved wilderness land from 9.1 million to 105

---

[66] 'Bonobo Credo: Make love not war', Bonobo Initiative, http://www.bonobo.org/peace.html, viewed on 14 December 2007
[67] James Heartfield, 'Two Cheers for Agri-Business', *Review of Radical Political Economics,* 32, 2, 2000, p. 321
[68] World Wildlife Fund, http://www.worldwildlife.org/forests/pubs/ARPA_Comp_FS.pdf, viewed on 14 December 2007

million acres. Together with national parks and ungrazed forest land, fully 623 million acres, a quarter of the nation's land mass was excluded from development in 1990.[69] By 2002 that had increased to 759,000,000 acres, one third of the country.[70]

The United Nations lists 102,102 protected areas covering 18,763,407 km^2 or 12.65 per cent of the Earth's surface, more than the combined area of China and Southeast Asia. Since 1962 the protected area of the world has grown by more than seven times.

Protected areas in World Parks Congress

Year	Number	Area, million km^2
1962	9,214	2.4
1972	16,394	4.1
1982	27,794	8.8
1992	48,388	12.3
2003	102,102	18.8

The general view of greedy logging companies, agri-businesses and developers cutting down the forests is quite wrong – almost 180 degrees wrong. In truth farmland in particular is contracting. Across the world the land given over to grain harvesting shrunk from 732 million hectares in 1981 to 656 million in 2000 (after growing solidly from 587 million in 1950). Over the same years, grain yields from each hectare grew from 1.1 tons to 2.7 tons. Better farming methods, boosted output, so that less land was needed to grow more grain.

In fact the increase in grain production is the reason why land is being retired from farm use.

---

[69] The Wilderness Act of 1964, http://www.wilderness.org/OurIssues/Wilderness/act.cfm, viewed on 14 December 2007

[70] Major Uses of Land in the United States, 2002/EIB-14, Economic Research Service/USDA, p 4

After years of growth, grain stores were overflowing in the western world. In Europe the leftover output was so great that the EU had to buy it up. Their excess was called the butter mountain, the beef mountain and the wine lake. American farmers had their waste grain bought under Public Law 480, under which it was dumped on the Third World as 'Aid'. The waste was obscene – and seen as such. Commissioner Ray MacSharry changed the European Union's farming laws. Instead of giving farmers money to grow more grain, they gave them money to set aside land. The current area under obligatory set-aside amounts to 3.8 million hectares [38,000 km^2] in the EU.[71]

When at the end of the last century, farm prices continued to fall, the British government made its advice clear – 'we will support new opportunities to diversify', or in plain language, get out of farming if you can.[72] The government made grants available to farmers to get into niche markets like organic food – £30,853,887 was paid out between 2002 and 2007 to convert 711,223 hectares to lower yield organics.[73] As well as reducing output by turning farmers to organics, government turned more land to national parks – including those at Loch Lomond and the Trossachs (1,865 km^2 since 2007), the New Forest (570 km^2, since 2005) and the Cairngorms (38,000 km^2, since 2007) with the South Downs already proposed to follow (currently 1602 km^2 proposed).

Retiring farmland might seem like a rational policy to manage overall food supply. If too much food is being produced then production out to be reduced. But it should be borne in mind that this is not a case of matching the supply of farm produce to satisfy world hunger. Agribusiness, and governments are only interested in seeing *effective* demand satisfied, not *absolute* demand. What matters to them

---

[71] IP/07/1402, Brussels, 26 September 2007, http://europa.eu/rapid/pressReleasesAction.do?aged=0&format=HTML&guiLanguage=en&language=EN&reference=IP/07/1402, viewed on 14 December 2007 Europe has an area of 10,355,000 sq km

[72] Department of the Environment, Transport and the Regions, *Our Countryside – the future*, London, HMSO, November 2000, p. 91

[73] DEFRA, Organic Farming Statistics, http://www.defra.gov.uk/erdp/schemes/ofs/ofsstatistics.htm, viewed on 14 December 2007

is not whether people are hungry, but whether they are willing and able to buy the goods. Reducing output when millions are still undernourished is a perverse policy of engineering scarcity to secure agribusiness' profits.

Engineering the retirement of farmland is largely a way of easing small farmers (who had been protected under the old Common Agricultural Policy) out of farming altogether. It has not hurt the larger agribusinesses, which are thriving. Not surprisingly, farm goods are a target for speculators, like seventies corporate raider, Jim Slater, whose new Agra Firma was started up to take advantage of booming prices. The reduction in excess output has in the last few years pushed prices up again, after long decades of falling food prices. In Italy, consumers boycotted pasta because prices rose so high; in Mexico, Tortilla Rallies protested against price rises, and in India there have been onion demonstrations.[74] The *Economist* estimates that food prices rose by one third in the year to December 2007 (having fallen by three quarters between 1975 and 2005).[75] According to the mainstream media, the pressure of biofuels and global warming are to blame for the shortfall in crops – as if governments had not been involved in a twenty-year programme of retiring land from production. Today's scarcities have been engineered, in the name of saving the environment, but in fact to defend the livelihoods of big agriculture.

The 'Green Belt' choking off new homes

In the twelve years from 1995 to 2007 house-building in Britain slumped to its lowest since 1945. The yearly average was 180,000, which is to say too few to replace the houses we have, let alone house the estimated growth of an additional four million households. When demand grew and supply was cut prices went through the roof. Average house prices rose from £60,000 to £200,000 between 1995 and 2007.[76]

---

[74] Jonathan Watts, 'Riots and hunger feared as demand for grain sends food costs soaring,' *Guardian,* 4 December 2007
[75] 'Cheap no more', *Economist,* 6 December 2007
[76] http://www.houseprices.uk.net, viewed on 17 October 2007

The limits on the output of the construction industry were not undertaken to boost prices – that was just a symptom. Rather, wealthy people tried to shore up the exclusive value of their homes by limiting nearby building. The reason for the slump in housebuilding was a powerful anti-growth coalition of environmentalists and 'not in my back yard' (Nimby) homeowners. Worse still, this lobby, which once would have been faced down by government, was instead handed control over housing policy. The Campaign to Protect Rural England, English Heritage, The Green Party and anti-Roads Protestors all found common ground opposing the building of new homes. The government gave housing policy to an Urban Task Force that gave full vent to the anti-growth prejudices.[77]

In 1996 the City of Portland in Oregon adopted its Region 2040 plan with the slogan 'grow up not out'. The plan reinforced the green belt Portland adopted in 1973.[78] Its plan was to save countryside from suburban sprawl. From now on Portland would have 'smart growth'. The result was densification of the centre, but also climbing house prices as fewer were built to satisfy demand. Estimates of house price hikes vary between $10,000 and $35,000.[79]

Though only 0.25 per cent of Australia is developed, its state governments have adopted 'smart growth' restrictions so that thirty times as much land is protected (as national parks and so on) as is occupied. As a result house prices had risen to 8.5 times the median income in Sydney by 2005, six times that in Melbourne, Brisbane, Perth Adelaide and Hobart.[80] The rationale behind the growth restrictions was described by Michael Duffy in the *Sydney Morning Herald:* 'To see mere tradesmen in the 1980s acquiring bigger houses than those owned

---

[77] See James Heartfield, *Let's Build! Why we need five million new homes in the next 10 years,* London, Audacity, 2006

[78] Robert Bruegmann, *Sprawl: a compact history,* Chicago, University Press, 2005, p 204-6

[79] Wendell Cox, *War on the Dream,* Lincoln, iUniverse, 2006, p 142-3

[80] Second Annual Demographia Survey, Belleville, Demographia, 2006

by many lawyers and academics sent a shiver through the middle class, and helped create an audience for absurd criticisms of prole housing'.[81]

In Britain the government's Urban Task Force, chaired by Sir Richard Rogers, advised strict enforcement of green belts and a new policy of building only on derelict 'brownfield' land: the 'build up not out' policy.

At the core of this campaign against growth was an ill-disguised hatred for mass housing – particularly focussed on the despised 'suburban' sprawl. Once the wealthy could rely on their monopoly over land to hold up the division between the rich man in his castle and the poor man at his gate. But the liberalisation of financial markets and rising incomes meant working-class people could aspire to own their own homes.

That much was an anathema to the stockbroker belt snobs, who just did not want to see Essex man extend his realm into Suffolk and Winchester. They were joined by the nervous burghers of London and other major cities who were scared that the masses would escape their overpriced and under-resourced inner city redoubts.

Unable to prevent the 'human sprawl' by economic means, they have leant on extra-economic, legal and political restraints: planning law and other 'smart growth' restrictions. Just as working people got their hands on enough money to buy houses, the green lobby, the Shire Tories and the Town Hall bureaucrats got together to use the law to stop the masses getting away.

Restrictions on housing sprawl created denser cities, seeing the return of overcrowding in some parts of London.[82] But overall its impact was to limit the supply of homes. This piece of manufactured scarcity transferred wealth from poor to rich, as homeowners saw the value of their assets climb, while younger families paid out more and

---

[81] 'Suburbs attacked because middle class hates plumbers in big houses', *Sydney Morning Herald*, 27 October 2007

[82] Ironically, the 'brownfield' development rule means that what new homes are being built are indeed being built in back yards – in cities. The BBC reports 'garden grabbing': 'a rash of flats and new houses replacing gardens in high-price areas'. Finlo Rohrer, 'One day all this will be multi-occupancy units', http://news.bbc.co.uk:80/1/hi/magazine/6744797.stm, viewed on 14 December 2007

more in mortgage repayments or rent. Estate agents made a fortune as their commissions climbed, and the volume housebuilders discovered they could just as easily make money making fewer homes at a higher price as more homes more cheaply. Even with low output Barratt and David Wilson, who make nearly half of all new homes in Britain, enjoy healthy profit rates of 47 per cent.

Sir Peter Hall estimated the amount by which an acre of land increased in price once its owners had been granted planning permission under the Town and Country Planning Act – 'planning gain': 'the windfall gain that a landowner makes on the grant of planning permission – which, in the case of conversion of farmland to residential use, can mean an uplift from £3,800 to £1 million an acre.'[83] This planning gain is not a reward for new development, but a windfall profit created by a state-imposed monopoly on planning permission. There is of course no natural scarcity in land for houses. Land use surveys tell us that only one tenth of the UK is built-up, and of the three quarters of the country dedicated to farming, around a third, because of overproduction, is not needed and should be made available for dwellings. But instead of releasing land for people, the government reserves more and more of the retired farm land for national parks, areas of scientific interest and other fictional justifications for manufacturing scarcity in land for housing.

---

[83] Peter Hall, 'What PGS could bring to the end of the party', *Town and Country Planning,* September 2007, p. 283

5. GREEN CONSUMERISM

Considering that greens have railed against the consumer society, it is remarkable just how much they have stoked it up. Green thinking has generated wants that people never knew they had.

Organic vegetables, solar panels, bottled mineral water, electric cars, windmills, tofu, solar powered calculators, fair-trade chocolate, low-energy electric bulbs, water purifiers, 'Dorothy' vegetarian shoes, quinoa, corn-fed chicken, dried mango snacks, miso, GM-free soy, 'I am not a plastic bag' bags, air purifiers, reusable nappies, hybrid cars, non-animal tested cosmetics, juicing machines, bagged and washed salad – these are just some of the goods that have been developed to meet the growing needs of the environmentally-aware shopper. The irony that this new raft of wants has helped to stoke up additional consumer demand, and made supermarkets even more money than they were already making, has not escaped the more tortured green commentators.[84] That much of the organic food sold is flown in means its so-called 'carbon footprint' is often estimated to be larger than for conventional foods (and, as we shall see, there are other reasons that organics represent a greater drain on resources).

Ethical shopping flatters us that our everyday buying is doing good. As activism goes, it is pretty easy. This is politics for slackers. We do not have to give up very much – just go shopping for the right stuff.

Still, there is nothing wrong in principle with these new consumer demands. Shops are not there to make us better people – who could agree what a better person is? – shops are just there to give us the things we want. Many of those wants are just part of the ordinary enlargement of human desire. Why not dried cranberries? Some wants, of course arise out of our particular hang-ups in the here-and-now.

---

[84] Mark Lynas, 'The Green Shopping Con', *Guardian,* G2 17 September 2007

Often these wants are intuitive reactions to that vague background belief that the modern world is poisoning us. Evian mineral water, for example, trades on an unstated mistrust of the water utilities – though by any standard, ecological, economic or just ergonomic, bottled water is a less efficient than piped. The label might show a stream, but water pipes are a better approximation of one than bottles, which are the modern equivalent of stagnant ponds. All the same, it makes little sense to argue with people's purchasing choices: they are the people they are, and their needs are psychological as well as biological.

Also, there is little point in lecturing people about what they should and should not want, because quite enough of that goes on already. Government edicts, health authority guidelines, food-labelling rules, municipal promotion programmes, right down to school lessons all drum home a distinctive message: people should eat healthier, more natural foods, drive less, shop ethically, recycle and save energy. Lots of people are simply exhausted by constant ticking off. One quarter of those polled in the UK thought that it takes too much effort to do things that are environmentally friendly, and a similar number did not believe that their behaviour and everyday lifestyle contribute to climate change. Half found that there were no practical alternatives to car use and one third did not really want to drive or fly less.[85] On the very broadest definition of 'ethical shopping' – air-mile laden fair trade goods alongside solar panels – British households gave just four per cent of their yearly £600 billion spending to it.[86]

Ethical shopping is status affirmation

Reluctant environmentalists are not the most important market segment to green retailers. Retailers understand that 'early adopters' of buying trends influence wider tastes. What the few ethically-minded shoppers were doing fifteen years ago – buying organic food for example – was

---

[85] 'Millions say it is too much effort to adopt greener lifestyle', *Guardian*, 15 August 2007
[86] 'Ethical Household spending...' *Guardian*, 30 November 2007

adopted by wider groups later on. In recent times green consumers have been driving the market. That is because green purchasing is status affirmation. Buying green marks out consumers not just as ethically minded, but more ethically minded than others. Even more than most consumer trends, green consumer power is about social demarcation. Green goods are directly contrasted to mass consumer goods. Their identity is asserted against less ethical, mass produced goods.

In 2007 the *Ecologist* magazine's competition to name examples of modern ugliness got readers' dander up. The green fogies rounded on 'new housing estates', 'children's food', supermarkets (the Rochdale Asda being the worst), bagged salad and litter. Their pet hates were revealing. Other people buying stuff is upsetting to the greens. Their ecology is all about setting themselves apart from the mass, by their ecologically aware purchases.

Funnily enough, green thinking makes more, not less consumption. It could be stated as an economic law: the greener you are, the more you consume. If that seems a bit hard to swallow, let's break it down. First, the richer you are, the greener you are. Second, the richer you are, the more you consume.

All the surveys show the same thing, higher income correlates with greater environmental consciousness.[87] Environmental activism correlates with higher income, too.[88] That is not just true on an individual level. Those parts of the world that are greener in outlook are also those that are wealthier.[89] Districts that elect green representatives tend to be wealthier, like Brighton, Reading, North Devon and Oxford in Britain; California, Maine and Pennsylvania in the US.[90] Environmental consciousness has become greater, just as consumption has become greater. Green thinking is the religion of the consumer age.

---

[87] M. Aytulk Kasapoglu and Mehmet Ecevit, 'Attitudes and behaviour towards the Environment', *Environment and Behavior,* Vol. 34, No. 3, 363-377 (2002), p374;
[88] Jowell, R. et al. (eds) *British and European Social Attitudes: How Britain Differs: The 15th Report,* Aldershot, Ashgate Publishing, 1998 p 132
[89] Ronald Inglehart and Paul Abramson, *Value Change in Global Perspective,* Michigan, University Press, 1995, p. 123-127
[90] Green Party of the United States, 'Green Office Holders' http://www.gp.org/elections/GreenOfficeholders-2007-09-27.xls, viewed on 14 December 2007

Of course, greens would say that they are protesting *against* consumerism. And so they are. But the way that it really works is that greens protest against a certain kind of consumption – mass consumption. By their green consumer choices, environmentalists are demonstrating that they are better than the herd. What we have instead is green consumerism. Green consumerism does not mean consuming less than the rest. In fact it ends up meaning that you consume more. Your consumer choices are more finicky, less easily satisfied. They say something about you. They say that you are 'concerned about the planet'. The say you are more discerning. But most of all they say that you are wealthier than the people down the street.

Of course there might be one or two deep greens who live like monks. There was the Unabomber, Ted Kaczynski, who lived in a hut in the woods. And then there is Mayer Hillman, who cycles around London, with a flask. But most of those who promote the green lifestyle live high on the hog, like Al Gore, Leonardo DiCaprio or Zac Goldsmith.

Organic food: an early example of the way that green goods are status goods.

Organic food was first promoted in health food shops. It is more expensive than comparable foods. Its buyers were food faddists – a more exclusive group than today's TV-chef enlarged 'foodies'. As a social groups they were for the most part middle class enough to want to differentiate themselves from the mass, but not rich enough to distinguish themselves by high end luxury goods. Their fastidious lifestyles – bread-making, Aga cookers, ethnic clothes, Volkswagen beetle cars or 2CV Renaults (with 'Nuclear Power, no thanks!' stickers), unvarnished pine furniture were mocked at the time but in time have influenced consumer habits markedly (think Ikea, Bodyshop, grunge). In 1962, Rachel Carson wrote a book called *Silent Spring,* about the supposed dangers of DDT and pesticides entering the food chain. The book was a favourite among the faddists who were already up in arms about fluoride in the water supply and so embraced the new, pesticide-free organic farming.

The broader take up in organic food was kick-started by a succession of food panics: junior minister Edwina Currie overreacted to the possibility of salmonella poisoning in eggs leading to a collapse in sales; then government scientist Robert Lacey warned that one third of Britons would become infected with CJD – 'the human form of BSE' (Bovine Spongiform Encephalopathy) leading to a collapse in beef farming and mass cull; then just as beef herds recovered a foot and mouth outbreak seemed to confirm the belief that factory farming was teeming with disease.

Largely urban, the reaction against factory farming in the wake of the BSE crisis reinforced the anxiety about food that had launched organic farming. Though collapse in beef sales was universal, the food scares re-emphasized middle class disgust at fast foods, especially McDonalds hamburgers. Middle-class protesters picketed McDonalds and the Piccadilly store was ransacked by angry anti-capitalist protesters in 1999.

Organic food sales have risen remarkably. Together with free range and fair trade food its sales reached £2 billion. Research analysts Mintel said that the growth represented 'increased disposable incomes and changing customer attitudes'.[91] Those sales, however, still represent less than two per cent of all food sold in Britain, whose value is £109 billion.[92]

The organic food trade is promoted by the Soil Association of organic farmers. Organic farming expanded as an alternative to farmers who were caught in a price squeeze as the success of their industry led to a glut in the market. To avoid the race to the bottom in farm prices, organic farmers have managed to realise a premium based upon anxieties about safety and social status. But refusing chemical pesticides does mean that organic farms are less productive, and their

---

[91] *Guardian,* 13 October 2006
[92] Family Food in 2005-6, National Statistics, p 5
http://statistics.defra.gov.uk/esg/publications/efs/2006/chapter1.pdf , viewed on 14 December 2007. Weekly food per person = £35, or £1820 annually, times 60 million persons.

goods correspondingly more expensive. To the irritation of the Soil Association, the Food Standards Agency insists that organic food is no safer than non-organic.

The success of the organic food revolution, however, has brought anxieties that it is being taken over by big business. The US supermarket chain Whole Foods Market turns over $6 billion a year, and is under attack because it is not exclusive enough: 'whole foods lite'. Author Michael Pollan pointed out the obvious when he said that a business with a turnover measured in billions is hard-headed capitalism.[93] Much to the Soil Association's dismay, retailers in Britain buy in 47 per cent of their organic produce from abroad,[94] and so the SA are considering taking the organic label off food with 'air-miles'.

Air travel – the hypocrisy of the conscientious consumer

Environmental writer George Monbiot says that 'flying across the Atlantic is as unacceptable, in terms of its impact on human well-being, as child abuse'.[95] Monbiot outs Coldplay lead singer Chris Martin, concerned about how people 'treat the planet', as owner of his own private jet, while one unnamed climate-change campaigner 'spends her holidays snorkelling in the Pacific'. But why not name names? Friends of the Earth director Tony Juniper flew to Malaysia, South Africa, Amsterdam and Nigeria in 2006, as well as taking his family on holiday to Slovakia. In the same month that she was seeking to legislate against the airline industry, Green MEP Caroline Lucas was flying to India; Al Gore's frequent use of private jets to campaign and promote An Inconvenient Truth are extensive. Ashok Sinha flew to India and Montreal while he was organising the Stop the Climate Chaos protest.[96] Zac Goldsmith reluctantly admits to flying 'once this year' while Monbiot himself quietly acknowledges 'the occasional flights I take— hypocritically or paradoxically, depending on your point of view—in

---

[93] *Guardian*, 27 March 2007
[94] *Guardian*, 14 November 2005
[95] *Guardian*, 29 July 1999
[96] 'A green snag they omitted to mention', *Sunday Times*, 1 October 2006

order to speak about climate change in other countries'.[97] (Was there nobody more local who could have made the same points, or perhaps a video-link?)

> The climate change debate is a 'middle class, mid-life crisis', Michael O'Leary, Ryanair Chief Executive.[98]

You might think that foregoing air travel was a small price to pay to if you really thought that it was destroying the planet – or indeed if you wanted to say with any authority that we have to make sacrifices to save it. But that would be to misunderstand the importance of air travel for the Green Elite. Pretentious as it is, this piece of ad-speak from BBC World's John Howlett is describing a real market demographic:

> The Internationalists are the new-age citizens who are populating today's world. They are the decision-drivers, avid travelers, big spenders and conscientious consumers. They are global influencers and early adopters who are committed to global issues…[99]

The 'conscientious consumers' love air travel – for themselves. They just hate cheap air travel that everyone else can enjoy. The reason they first got into tourism was to get away from us. Now that we are all following them, ruining their isolated spots in Ibiza and the Dordogne, they need a reason to stop us. Not to put too fine a point on it, concern over CO_2 emissions came *after* the prejudice that mass tourism was a

---

[97] 'Environmental Feedback', *New Left Review,* 45, May 2007, p 112; 'I have flown twice in the past three years, on both occasions to talk about climate change. I believe it was justified.' Contribution to 'Live online Q & A with George Monbiot', 01:17pm Jun 20, 2007 at www.guardian.co.uk. Monbiot's co-author on the book *Heat: how to stop the planet burning,* Mark Lynas 'was selected by *National Geographic* as one of its Emerging Explorers' for his book High Tide, and 'has given talks and presentations on climate change and his travels for *High Tide* as far away as the United States and Australia' according to his *Guardian* 'Comment is Free' Profile.
[98] *Guardian,* 6 November 2007
[99] Quoted in *Private Eye,* 12 October 2007

blight. Global warming predictions provide a useful, quasi-scientific justification for anti-working class prejudice.

'When I challenge my friends about their planned weekend in Rome or their holiday in Florida, they respond with a strange, distant smile and avert their eyes' writes Monbiot, 'the moral dissonance is deafening'[100] It is a good description of the disconnect between lecturing the rest of us about our unworthy travel and Monbiot's own necessary trips in the belly of the beast. But then the moral injunction against Easyjet was never meant to apply to 'conscientious consumers'. It was designed to clear the skies of short haul tourists so that the New Internationalists would not be offended by the sight of sun-burnt football fans boozing on the beach.

The Green consumer's dilemma

Commentaries on green buying often talk up just how difficult it is to be green. Green consuming is a dilemma. Why? The short answer is that green ideals are themselves incoherent, and naturally give rise to all kinds of conundrums.

Part of the ambiguity is the question what is it exactly that you are saving. Depending on which resource it is that is in jeopardy, your consumer preferences will be different. If oil is at a premium, then bio-fuels make sense – but less so if it is land that is supposed to be in short supply, because bio-fuels take up land. If the well being of African small producers ought to be saved, then Fair Trade is a good idea, but if CO_2 emissions are the problem, then the Soil Association was right to refuse Fair Trade goods their stamp of approval. If neighbourliness is what the modern world lacks then the corner shop might be the answer, but if the problem is greenhouse gases then perhaps Tesco's deliveries are a more CO_2 efficient way to get your shopping.[101] Still worse, former Greenpeace activist Dr Patrick Moore points out that France and

---

[100] 'For the sake of the world's poor, we must keep the wealth at home', *Guardian*, 28 February 2006
[101] As George Monbiot reluctantly concedes in his book *Heat*, London, Penguin, 2006, p. 197

Sweden have the lowest CO_2 footprints in western Europe, because most of their electricity is nuclear-generated.[102] And if it is the climate that is at risk, then we ought to be willing to sacrifice England's green and pleasant land to the march of the wind farm.

> From **The Keeper of Flocks**, XXVIII
>
> *Talking about the soul of stones, of flowers, of rivers,*
> *Is talking about yourself and your false thoughts.*
> *Thank God stones are only stones,*
> *And rivers are nothing but rivers,*
> *And flowers are just flowers.*
>
> *Me, I write the prose of my poems*
> *And I'm at peace,*
> *Because I know I comprehend Nature on the outside;*
> *And I don't comprehend Nature on the inside*
> *Because Nature doesn't have an inside;*
> *If she did she wouldn't be Nature.*
>
> Alberto Caeiro da Silva, 1914

There is of course no way to settle these competing dilemmas because at its heart green thinking is not a coherent ideology but a rag-bag of knee-jerk prejudices. The problem is that nature is not singular, but multi-form. It offers up a great variety of different shapes and structures, none of which has any priority. As such it lacks a uniting principle, which could be elevated above all others. Only man can unify nature, either rationally, as a store of resources, or romantically, as a fantastic projection of the ego. The vague green sentiment that all is not

---

[102] Sweden, which generates half its electricity in nuclear power stations, the other half hydro-electrically, has the lowest carbon footprint, France which generates 80 per cent of its electricity through nuclear power, the second lowest. Dominic Rushe, 'The man behind the nuclear power shift'. *Sunday Times,* Business Section, 2 December 2007.

right with the modern world can be worked up into detailed prognoses like climate change, land pressure or the social deficit. But however systematic each of these diagnoses is, the green sentiment is not reducible to any one of them. Each can be jettisoned or picked up in turn without damage to the core prejudice that modern life is exhausting nature's bounty.

The real dilemma goes deeper. It is not possible to generalise the green lifestyle. By definition, an ideology that sees mass consumption as the problem cannot be adopted by the masses. If all food were organic, the reduced yields would exhaust the world's land supply. The only point of organic food is that it sets the ethical consumer apart from the mass. Once supermarkets start to stock it, the status it confers is compromised. The green belt is a barrier designed to stop the 'sprawl' of volume housing from disturbing the green village idyll.

Luckily for the green retailers, capitalism thrives on contradiction. Shopping does not have to make sense. Impulse buying, not forward planning, is what counts in the supermarket. Health food shoppers might be quietly appalled to see their habits aped by Tesco's clientele, and move on to a more complex code of exclusive purchasing. That is no problem. Today's luxury goods have always provided the template for tomorrow's mass consumer items. The elite's restless pickiness is a spur to product innovation.

6. THE ECONOMY OF WASTING TIME

Today's green capitalism has turned many core assumptions of business on their head. One of the most important is the changed attitude to the productivity of labour. The measure of labour productivity is output, divided by hours (or days) spent. The long-term trend has been for a continuous reduction in labour-time per item. Business used to put great store by reducing the time spent on making goods. Of course, we all understood that they did not do it to increase employees' leisure time. Instead they did it to cut wage costs. When wages were high, that was a pressing need. The transformation of capitalism in recent times, though, has undermined that need. Because wages are lower, you cannot save as much money as you used to be able to by cutting jobs. There is less incentive to shed labour. In fact it is so cheap, that businesses are more likely to hang on to employees.

Overall the trend has been towards labour-intensive growth – making more by putting more people to work, rather than by making more in less time. In the UK labour productivity actually fell over the last four years, because more people were working in less productive service industries than in more productive manufacturing.

Governments responded to the social problem of unemployment in the 1980s by trying to fill people's time with expanded further education and training schemes. Governments addressed the problem they called 'social exclusion' by trying to get more people to work. That was not easy, at first. The French government made special jobs for young people. In Britain legislators increased nursery provision to persuade more mothers back to work.

Low-paying, service sector employment boomed in part because governments wanted it to soak up surplus labour. But at the same time employers were more likely to hang on to people now that wages were held down. Hours, after rising sharply in the 1980s, began to fall again as the balance of the workforce became more feminised, and more service-sector oriented.

In fact, employers, who were once vigilant saving every spare minute at work, now began to waste their employees' time. More and more time was filled with in-house training, team-building activities, like white-water rafting or paint-balling that were promoted by the new human resource managers.

The initial motivation for these time-wasting activities was to keep employees interested, especially when the wage reward was less compelling. Human Resources created artificial career structures to supplement the loss of meaningful goals. In-house training joined team-building activities as a way of re-engaging with employees' subjectivity.

But often the goal was nothing more than keeping employees occupied during unavoidable downtime. In the 1990s, the advertising agency St Luke's got a groovy reputation for doing right-on *pro bono* work. It was a good answer to the view that advertising was a business without morals, but it was also a convenient way to keep the creatives engaged in lean times. Where employers did not engage their staff, managers would turn a blind eye to absenteeism. At the BBC, as much as one twentieth of the workforce would be off on 'gardening leave' at any moment, simply because they had no project to work on.

In the United States employees told researchers that they waste around two hours a day surfing the internet and socialising – time that represented some $759 billion lost to business.[103] Non-work activities at work include phoning friends, playing solitaire or browsing the internet, reading, raising funds for charities, picking up and dropping off kids at school, attending parents' evenings, and exercising, often at work-provided facilities.[104]

As much as private business, government had its ways of wasting people's time. In 1998, the British government set out to waste motorists' time with so-called 'traffic-calming' measures – in fact a series of modifications to the road system to slow down traffic, including traffic humps, lane reductions and re-scheduled traffic

---

[103] *Guardian,* 12 July 2005
[104] W. Michael Cox and Richard Alm, *Myths of Rich and Poor: why we're better off than we think.* New York, Basic, Books 1999, p. 67

signalling – all on the principle of reducing road use. In practice these only added to commuting time, tying up motorists for 45 minutes each day in manufactured congestion that is increasing by as much as five per cent each year.[105]

After decades spent ruthlessly cutting time-wasting in industry (1939-1990) and more recently forcing up working hours (1980-88) this recent and surprising involution of the Protestant work ethic shows just how much modern capitalism has changed. Instead of saving labour time as it did until very recently, today society is squandering it. And here, intriguingly, the environmental ethos fits in nicely with the time-wasting trend.

Environmental writers have identified speed as one of the great problems of our time, proposing instead the adoption of 'slow living'. Downshifting has become a modern, middle-aged version of dropping out. In France the Slow Town movement has taken off, mirrored in Britain by Transition Towns (looking forward, or backward, to an age without fossil fuels).

Pointedly, environmental economists aim to save every imaginable resource – land, energy, topsoil, water, the ozone layer – but one. Tellingly, damningly, the one expendable resource in the green canon, is man himself. The appropriate technology campaign promotes inefficient, labour intensive tools over newer technologies. The recycling campaigns squander billions of hours of human labour time recovering relatively small amounts of paper, waste-food and tin.
The lesson of recycling is that environmentalism holds every resource more precious than our time. That is hardly surprising. The philosophy of environmentalism elevates nature over man. Squandering our lives in meaningless rituals of ecological concern is the natural conclusion of environmentalism. More remarkable is that, in its dotage, capitalism has come to share this destructive attitude.

---

[105] 'The 45-minute commute', *Independent,* 22 July 2003; 'Queue the irritation', *Observer,* 26 October 2003

> **Recycling is a waste of time**
>
> Local authority recycling initiatives force rubbish sorting onto households, though anyone can see that this is labour inefficient. Councils provide households with different coloured bins for cardboard and paper, kitchen and general waste.
>
> Lacking the means to enforce common agreement on the definition of the different categories of waste, refuse departments commonly re-sort domestically sorted waste, centrally.
>
> More often, recycling schemes are simply a sham, as in Norfolk, where the local authority simply threw the domestically– sorted waste together into landfill (http://news.bbc.co.uk/1/hi/england/2293163.stm).
>
> In March 2005 Dutch authorities intercepted British household rubbish, domestically separated, but reunited in 60 containers destined for China, where it was to be sorted a second time (http://news.bbc.co.uk/1/hi/programmes/real_story/4490056.stm, Guardian, 4 April 2005). According to the Environment Agency, about half of the 8m tons of green bin material thrown out each year in the UK ends up overseas, mainly in China and Indonesia.
>
> Kerbside recycling collections cost anywhere between £100 and £1000 a tonne, and the Welsh Assembly subsidised local authority collections to the tune of £42 million in 2006-7 (*Survey of Funding of Municipal Waste Management Kerbside Collection in Wales,* 2007). Still, additional costs have led many authorities to cut back weekly collections to fortnightly ones. In Oxford and elsewhere, these cuts are blamed for outbreaks of rats and other vermin.
>
> Though these schemes are popular with local authorities, they generally prove to be more costly than effective. Unable to command consistency from voluntary household sorting, only third world labour is cheap enough to make the operation worthwhile, leading to the bizarre result that waste is shipped thousands of miles to be sorted. The net result is a squandering of human energies in pursuit of a chimerical ecological saving.

Capitalism was always a combined system pursuing production but also social control. Just as they were dragooned into the army, press-ganged onto ships, indentured to plantations, labourers – or 'hands' – were marshalled into factories to be put under supervision. But at least under the old capitalism, social control had as a by-product an enlarged industrial base and a greater mass of consumer goods. Under the new, green capitalism, the overriding goal is the absorption of human abilities irrespective of their usefulness, and increasingly a fruitless squandering of those resources in make-work schemes.

Reversing the division of labour

Adam Smith identified the 'division of labour' as the great advance of the factory age. Even before machinery substituted for motive power, industry increased human effort many times over, just by sub-dividing complex tasks among many. Where craftsmen were Jacks-of-all trades, the factory hand mastered one. Just by putting men under the same roof, great economies of scale were made, and human industry released from the endless reproduction of effort that came with domestic production. Instead of being dissipated, effort was concentrated. Specialised businesses for making shoes, engines, even power itself, were bound to be more efficient than attempts to achieve the same on the basis of domestic industry.

Green economics takes us backwards, reinventing cottage industry. The 'self-sufficiency' prejudice of course is the very opposite of saving, but leads to a tremendous waste of energies and raw materials. But that does not stop greens embracing self-sufficiency. Domestic recycling reverses the division of labour. The job of rubbish sorting that was undertaken by refuse departments is put back in the home. Instead of one sorting depot, millions of kitchens and living rooms are given over to the job of sorting paper from tin, kitchen waste from paper. The reproduction of effort is astonishing. And being a cottage industry, domestic recycling's output is multiform, rendering it useless without further sorting, in a centralised depot.

We thought that Margaret Thatcher was testing the limits of market decentralisation when she privatised the ownership of electricity utilities. But Mrs Thatcher would never have dreamt of dispersing electricity production – and yet on 6 December 2007 Tory leader David Cameron took to the stage at the London Greenpeace offices to announce that he was aiming to 'decentralise energy generation'. In government, the Conservative Party would encourage homeowners to supply their own energy from renewable sources by installing wind turbines and solar panels. Reversing the division of labour in energy production is embraced as a policy goal across the developed world.

Domestic electricity generation with windmills and solar panels appeals to two subtly distinct aspirations. The first is energy efficiency. The second is energy self-sufficiency. The first might have a point – though the argument that solar power is superior to coal, gas, oil or nuclear generation is far from convincing. What is clear is that it makes no sense whatsoever to produce electricity in the home (any more than it does to bake your own bread, or carve your own clogs). *Self-sufficiency,* as opposed to *efficiency,* is a solipsistic prejudice buried in green thinking that is rarely made explicit but always there beneath the surface. The right-wing cult of survivalism always lurked behind BBC2's cheerful, grow-your-own comedy, *The Good Life.* Green dystopians love stories of the bitter fight for survival once the food runs out, like Cormac McCarthy's *The Road.*

Practically, domestic energy generation is bound to be less efficient than centralised electricity generation. Electricity is a difficult good to manage and training homemakers up to the standards required, and demanding the time of them, means taking them away from their useful contributions to the social division of labour. And yet the British government, like many of its European partners and American state governments subsidises the siting of solar panels in homes, workplaces and schools at great cost, and only intermittent success. The lion's share of these panels falls quickly into disuse, while the few that do operate absorb the energies of caretakers and householders without any realistic measure of what is lost when they abandon their other occupations.

As well as being a terrible waste of resources, David Cameron's policy of energy decentralisation would be unlikely to have a positive effect on greenhouse gas emissions: a Building Research Establishment Trust report found that home-based windmills very rarely generate enough electricity to offset the carbon emissions released in their production and installation – and usually not more than two per cent of household use.[106] But then the ever-cynical Tory leader knows full well that alternative energy generation is not efficient. His plan is wholly symbolic, to train the public to reduce consumption. As he explained 'once people start generating their own electricity, they will become far more conscious of the way in which they use it – they will become more responsible about energy use and their own environmental impact'.

The BedZed complex of flats built for the Peabody Trust was designed for energy and waste self-sufficiency, with the ambition of becoming 'zero-carbon'. Residents were not only tasked with energy generation, but water and waste management. Sewage was filtered through a reed bed (the 'living machine'), and energy generated from 'bio-mass' waste. What is more, no parking spaces were provided and a car-sharing scheme set up. Not surprisingly the car sharing foundered on the fact that the residents all worked in different places. Soon the sewage filtering failed, its novel technology depending on bespoke repairs by the architect, the reed bed stinking out the flats, showers running tepid. The bio-mass generator packed up, Peabody had to install traditional gas boilers and BedZed found itself dependent on the electricity companies.

BedZed's 'self-sufficiency' proved wholly inefficient. Opting out of the national division of labour in energy production – the National Grid – did not work. BedZed's cottage industry wasted more resources than it saved.

Two years ago, architect Bill Dunster was still pressing on, planning an organic farm in Kent where the tractors would run on rapeseed oil and, power would be generated by wind turbines and a methane biodigester CHP system. Electric delivery vehicles would bring the food to BedZed and Dunster's other urban communities in

---

[106] 'Micro-wind turbines often increase CO2, says study,' *Guardian,* 30 November 2007

London, the deliveries carbon food miles-free. These plans are absurd. If they were ever put into operation they would represent yet further squandering of resources, by throwing the existing division of labour in farming, energy and distribution into reverse. Creating another farm distribution network – a less efficient one – alongside the working model would be a pointless reproduction of efforts.

Until that plan comes to fruition, Dunster is making his money selling off-the-shelf energy 'efficiency' packages of solar panels, biomass machines and wind generators to over-ambitious householders. Twenty-first century snake oil. With an eye to the future he is talking to London Mayor Ken Livingstone about having environmental regulations written into planning law, so that new homes must install his products, and has bid for one of Prime Minister Brown's proposed 'eco-towns'.[107] BedZed's builders, the BioRegional Development Group are also bidding to build 'eco-towns' in Middlesborough, Brighton and the Thames Gateway, teaming up with FTSE-listed Quintain to bid for the £1.3 billion Wembley regeneration. Clearly, eco-failure is no barrier to economic success. Wasting resources is rewarded with new contracts.

In 2006, the New Economics Foundation launched its *UK Interdependence Report*. The report makes the argument for withdrawing the British economy from the international division of labour – a goal that would waste resources and efforts reproducing goods that can be made more efficiently elsewhere. The *Interdependence Report* identified *as a problem* the fact that the United Kingdom was increasingly dependent on other countries for its trade, energy and labour, as those other countries were dependent in turn upon the UK for capital export and new technologies. Of course it is right to look at questions of equity in international trade. But it would be quite wrong to consider the interchange of goods across national boundaries as a problem in itself. On the contrary, the international division of labour has been a great boon to human civilisation, as it should continue to be

---

[107] Terry Slavin, 'Building a Zero Carbon World', *Observer*, 13 August 2006

in the future.[108] Just as the BedZed development was an attempt to withdraw from the national economy in favour of domestic and local production the New Economics Foundation was making the case for withdrawing from the international division of labour in favour of national production. This Little Englander sentiment seems more plausible dressed in green, but it is still a beggar-thy-neighbour policy of protectionism that would simply waste people's energies doing things that can be done more efficiently elsewhere.

---

[108] see 'Interdependent we stand, divided we fall', Spiked-online.com, http://www.spiked-online.com/Articles/0000000CB035.htm, viewed on 14 December 2007

7. GREEN IMPERIALISM

More than most scientific questions, the state of the environment has been deeply mixed up with international rivalries. In fact, nations have politicised environmental claims as a weapon in their economic competition. CO_2 emissions mirror industrial output. Today's agreement to limit CO_2 emissions is nothing less than an attempt to regulate industrial competition.

The senior diplomat and former Coldstream Guard, Sir Crispin Tickell was one of the first people to identify the real-politik possibilities of ecological concern, in his book *Climate Change in World Affairs*. The book is a thinly-disguised justification for western-intervention into the internal domestic policies of newly-independent third world states. Those governments, wrote Tickell, 'can often make things as bad for their neighbours as for themselves... but they lack the knowledge and still more the means to cope'. It is telling that *Climate Change in World Affairs* was published in 1977, long before scientists identified global warming as a problem: Tickell used the perceived threat of smog as a justification for dictating terms to the developing world.

In 1988 Sir Crispin persuaded Prime Minister Margaret Thatcher to make a major speech on global warming as the 'new danger' that would replace the Soviet Threat as the motivation for Western policy. Eight years later, Thatcher, now in the role of eminence grise, repeated the point in a speech 'New Threats for Old' that is substantially modelled on an essay by Tickell.[109]

Finding a new principle around which to organise international diplomacy was pressing in the early nineties. For forty years the leading western powers had organised themselves, and the rest of the world in a campaign against Communism – but when Russia abandoned

---

[109] in Gwyn Prins (ed), *Threats Without Enemies: facing environmental insecurity*, London, Earthscan, 1993

Communism a new motivation had to be found for Western leadership in the world.

While most of the anti-capitalist protesters of today were still at school, the global elite put climate change on the agenda of the Rio Earth Summit, in June 1992, and agreed the United Nations Framework Convention on Climate Change at Kyoto in December 1997. Greenhouse gas emissions, which the Convention limits, roughly correspond to heavy industrial output, especially at a lower technological level. For that reason, different nations adopted differing stances to Kyoto, according to its differential impact. As a mature region, with declining growth rates, but a high technical level, Europe was pointedly in favour of the measure that set limits on its more dynamic competitors. Developing countries like Russia, India and China were pointedly more sceptical, as was the heavily producing United States. Indeed, China and India could only be persuaded to sign on the basis that they would not be subject to greenhouse gas limits under the principle of 'common but differentiated responsibilities.' Russia only agreed to sign up in exchange for membership of the World Trade Organisation. But despite negotiating opt-outs, the Kyoto framework makes their growth open to constant attack.[110] 'Developing nations whose emissions are surging are under no pressure to cut back', worries the *Sunday Times,* reporting that to 'bring India and China into a new emissions regime is a major part of what the EU and America wants to achieve [at the December 2007 climate change talks] at Bali'.[111]

The new climate deal struck at Bali lets first world countries offset *their* industrial growth by persuading less developed countries to forego growth, and enlarge their forest reserves instead. In effect the West will use its financial leverage to keep the natives sitting in darkness and its own monopoly on technology intact. Even Tony Juniper of Friends of the Earth was moved to denounce this deal as 'ecological imperialism foisted on the developing world'.[112]

---

[110] 'India and China urged to cut emissions', *Guardian* 28 August 2007
[111] Jonathan Leake, 'Carbon stand-off puts climate change talks at risk', *Sunday Times,* 9 December 2007
[112] *Guardian,* 12 December 2007

The debate over Kyoto made it clear that what was at issue was economic rivalry, masked as climate control. During the initial negotiations President Clinton was preoccupied with China and India, because 'within thirty years they would surpass the United States as emitters of greenhouse gases'.[113] Openly expressed, hostility to Chinese and Indian industrial expansion would sound like self-serving hypocrisy. Dressed up as environmental concern it looked like altruism. When the US Congress balked at reining in US industry and refused to sign Kyoto, it was America's turn to be attacked. The incoming US President was widely denounced by European protesters as 'The Toxic Texan'. Climate control makes national chauvinism acceptable.

For some radicals it seemed straightforward that the opponents of the Kyoto accord were industry spokesmen, and its defenders critics of big business. But that was to forget that capitalism is a competitive system. Setting limits to output was indeed a successful capitalist strategy, especially for those businesses with a lower carbon footprint, like banks and other financial speculators. Translated to competition at the international level, nations' interests differ according to the proportion of greenhouse-gas-emitting industries in their domestic economies. For those nations that are experiencing slower growth, penalising more dynamic competitors made sense. What is more, even for companies with higher emissions, raising the bar of entry could prove to be a successful business strategy. Of course, big greenhouse gas emitters were among the business lobby that opposed Kyoto, and the United States, being home to many of those, was among the most reluctant to sign up to the treaty. Was the Kyoto Convention, then, a blow against business? Hardly. Not if Enron, or the European Union, or Al Gore are to be counted among the enemies of big business.

Much more than any scientific advances, diplomatic wrangling set the terms of debate over climate change. The International Panel on Climate Change is perhaps the first scientific body to be organised by the United Nations rather than the academy. But the Convention on Climate Change is by no means the only example of economic warfare masquerading as environmentalism. When the US whaling business

---

[113] Bill Clinton, *My Life,* New York, Random House, 2005, p.770

declined post-war, the Independent Whaling Commission became the focus of anti-Japanese chauvinism enforcing a world ban on whaling nations (Japan, Iceland and Norway). To cope with its diplomatic isolation post-war, Germany became adept at promoting its interests through ecological politics, in such agreements as the 1987 Ministerial Declaration of the Second Conference of the Protection of the North Sea, which first established the 'vorsorgepinzip' or 'precautionary principle'.

EU-US economic rivalries are put in green words more and more. In the 1990s European farmers and environmentalists succeeded in lobbying the EU to embargo US food exports on the grounds that they were 'contaminated' with genetically modified organisms (GMOs). There is no health ground for fearing GMOs, but a concerted campaign by Greens convinced the European public that they were being made the guinea-pigs for a continent-wide Frankenfood experiment. As the evidence for the negative effects of GM failed to appear, Europeans remained committed to the barriers to US exports, convincing American negotiators like Robert Zoellick that the entire campaign was just greenwashed trade protection.

Setting limits on the developing world

Big power rivalry might be intense, but it is restrained. It is harder to push around powerful people than it is the less so. Countries in the developing world are at a much greater disadvantage. Third world nations did succeed in reining in the outright colonial domination that marked the nineteenth and twentieth centuries. Politically independent, they are still subject to western domination – though the West is constrained from proclaiming its authority too openly. As the emerging outlook of western elites, environmentalism is increasingly the idiom in which the claim to superiority is disguised. Environmental language makes western diktat to the developing world seem disinterested, rather than acquisitive. Western governments, aid agencies and NGOs ('non governmental organisations') pretend to be helping the environment, rather than hindering the peoples of the developing world.

In 1980, North-South – A Programme for Survival, the report of the Independent Commission on International Development Issues, dealt directly with the problem of the developed world's monopoly on technology. Under German Social Democrat and former premier Willy Brandt the report first popularised the case for 'appropriate technology' for the less developed world. Appropriate technology is a hybrid concept. It appeals both to the demand for better technology on the part of the people of the less developed world, and at the same time calls into question the generalisation of 'Western' technology.

Like the arguments for limits to growth, the Brandt report regretted that '…industrialised countries stick to a guiding philosophy which is predominantly materialistic and based on a belief in the automatic growth of gross national product'.[114] The point of the intervention was not in substance addressed to the developed world but the less so: 'We must not surrender to the idea that the whole world should copy the model of the highly industrialised countries'.[115]

It sounds like an argument for the underdog. The model of Western development is a bad one. But where does it take us? The West's monopoly over new technologies is intact. It is cute to pose this defence of the status quo as a critical doctrine, but it does not change its substance. By an act of ventriloquism, Brandt's commission puts the words 'those technology grapes are sour' into the mouths of the less developed world.

If the model of industrial development and growth is inappropriate for the South, what is appropriate? Here Brandt's commission becomes remarkably coy. The section on appropriate technology – the principle reason for which the report is remembered – is hedged around with caveats. In suggest that it is not for us to say what is and what is not appropriate. Yet appropriate technology 'can include cheaper sources of energy; simpler farm equipment; techniques in building, services and manufacturing processes which save capital;

---

[114] Independent Commission on International Development Issues *North-South: A Programme for Survival,* London, Pan, 1980, (henceforth, the Brandt Report), p. 24
[115] *The Brandt Report,* p. 23

smaller plants and scales of operation which can permit dispersal of activity'.[116]

What appropriate technology meant for the less developed world was the lowering of expectations; less capital input, less expenditure, less technology. Given the higher levels of consumption, life expectancy, natal survival, health care, air quality, nutrition, literacy and education, in the West, one might have thought that far greater levels of capital investment were appropriate for the South. But at its core, the argument over appropriate technology rested on an assumption that people in the South were just not expected to handle industrial growth.

The question was not theoretical. In real terms Western aid to developing countries came with conditions that limited development in the name of preserving the environment.

In November 2007 the European parliament resolved to withdraw all development aid for coal and oil powered industries. The overwhelming majority of European MPs voted for 'the discontinuation of public support, via export credit agencies and public investment banks, for fossil fuel projects' in the developing world. The vote slashed four billion euros worth of aid for industry in the least industrialised parts of the world. Around a half of all third world industry gets support from European export credits and the European Investment Bank – both of which are struck down by the vote.

While the EU cuts back on industrial production, what projects do western aid agencies support in the developing world?

- London-based Water Aid is pushing rope water pumps on reluctant Ghanaian villagers. Conceding that the initial uptake was small, Water Aid agreed that the rope often broke, the frame rusted and water was contaminated, but hoped these were just teething problems. In fact the villagers did not like the rope pump because it was worse than the powered pumps it replaced. But still western money recruited Ghanaian workers away from better technologies to this worse one.

---

[116] *The Brandt Report,* p. 195

- The United Nations' Regional Wood Energy Development Programme promotes wood-burning stoves as a friendlier alternative to oil-based heaters, along with partners like Journey to Forever: 'wood fuel is much more eco-friendly than more efficient and convenient fuels like kerosene'.[117] Every year, around five million young people die from respiratory diseases due to indoor wood smoke.
- Christian Aid invites you to give £344 to pay for two oxen, a plough and seed to help settle an Angolan farmer after the civil war, as they did for Domingas Noguera.[118] Meanwhile Oxfam has goats and bees that they cannot sell to Albanians and Africans, but can give them away, if you pay.[119]
- The Massachusetts Institute of Technology's D-Lab is supporting a Sari water filter, which, folded over just four times can reduce cholera infections by fifty per cent: 'The cloth is local, low-cost...it's an AT solution.'

The more primitive the kit, the more likely it is to get the funding.

Every year 1.8 million Africans die from malaria. Economist Jeffery Sachs estimates that malaria costs the continent 1.3 per cent growth each year. The most effective solution for malaria is to prevent the spread of disease-bearing mosquitoes by spraying with DDT. Unfortunately for Africa, US aid agencies have banned malarial DDT spraying since 1972 – influenced by Rachel Carson's scaremongering book *Silent Spring* (1962).[120]

Environmentalists have attacked a number of industrial projects in the developing world – because they do not think that it should develop. In January 2007 the Narmada Dam was opened in Gujarat,

---

[117] 'Wood fires that fit', Journey to Forever, http://journeytoforever.org/at_woodfire.html, viewed on 11 December 2007
[118] http://www.presentaid.org/invt/oxandplough, viewed on 11 December 2007
[119] http://www.oxfam.org.uk/shop/ProductDetails.aspx?catalog=Unwrapped&product=OU2731, viewed on 11 December 2007
[120] See Alex Gourevitch, 'Better living through chemistry', *Atlantic Monthly,* March 2003

generating 1450 megawatts of electricity, irrigating millions of acres and providing drinking water for thousands.[121] Because the dam displaced Narmada villagers, there were protests demanding proper resettlement and rehabilitation, led by the Arch-Vahini organisation.

The Narmada villagers were supported by Buddy Rich's Washington-based Environmental Defence Fund. But when Arch-Vahini agreed resettlement terms with the Gujarat government, the EDF turned on them, splitting the movement, creating their own breakaway Narmada Bachao Andolan ('Save the Narmada') in 1989. With the EDF's sponsorship, the NBA adopted an unrealistic programme of outright opposition to the dam. Villagers who accepted compensation packages were physically attacked by NBA supporters.

The EDF lobbied the World Bank and in 1993 the Bank withdrew its funding jeopardising the project. Another US-based NGO, the International Rivers Network, that was active in opposing the dam, explained their philosophy: 'A river is a thing of grace and beauty, a mystery and a metaphor, a living organism whose processes have been perfecting themselves through the ages, shaping our landscapes into works of art greater than those found in any museum.'[122] And on the basis of this mumbo-jumbo thousands were forced to live without electricity and running water. The American enemies of the Narmada Dam project were not making a considered point: they were *morally opposed* to dams as such. Years were wasted fighting a dam project whose overwhelming influence on Indian lives was for the good. Though they sought to speak through the mouths of indigenous residents, the real force behind the anti-dam protests was in Washington, and its greatest point of leverage was at the World Bank.

---

[121] Controversial Dam Launched, BBC Online 19 January 2007, http://news.bbc.co.uk/1/hi/world/south_asia/6278147.stm, viewed on 14 December 2007

[122] The case for rivers, International Rivers Network, http://www.irn.org/dayofaction/index.php?id=background5.html, viewed on 14 December 2007

> Grand Coulee Dam
>
> Uncle Sam took up the challenge in the year of '33
> For the farmer and the factory and all of you and me.
> He said, "Roll along Columbia. You can ramble to the sea,
> But river while you're ramblin' you can do some work for me."
> Now in Washington and Oregon you hear the factories hum,
> Making chrome and making manganese and light aluminum.
> And there roars a mighty furnace now to fight for Uncle Sam,
> Spawned upon the King Columbia by the big Grand Coulee Dam.
>
> Woody Guthrie

In the 1960s, agronomists like Cambridge Genetics graduate M.S. Swaminathan, and Iowa farmer Norman Borlaug developed the high yield strains of wheat and rice that laid the basis for a Green Revolution in India, China and Mexico. India's famines were at last over. But tragically for Africa, they missed the Green Revolution.

> There are 6.6 billion people on the planet today. With organic farming we could only feed 4 billion of them. Which 2 billion would volunteer to die? Norman Borlaug, Green Revolution pioneer[123]

By 1987 the United Nations was committed to another ideal 'sustainable development', as set out in Gro Harlem Brundtland's report, and building on Brandt's arguments for 'appropriate technology'. Being severely indebted (itself a consequence of the lower level of technological development Africa inherited from colonialism) African governments had to accept western strictures on how they should develop – even though these promoted traditional agriculture at the expense of their people.

---

[123] in Paul Driessen, *Eco-Imperialism,* Washington, Merril Press, 2004, p. 55

Crop[124]	World (Ave Yield: tones/ha)	Africa (Ave Yield: tones/ha)
Maize	4.1	1.7
Sweet potatoes	14.7	4.8
Bananas	48.1	6.0

In 2002, European Union officials used their loans as leverage to block US grain exports and aid to Africa. The purported reason for the ban was that some of the exports and aid were genetically modified. European farmers have successfully lobbied the EU to impose import restrictions on US farm produce. Then they sought to extend the ban. Because much of Africa's ex-colonies are dependent upon European subsidies under the Lomé agreement, they had little choice but to agree to the ban, even though they were denying their own people food.[125] Green campaigners vilified African agronomists who worked with GM technology, like Kenya's Dr. Florence Wambugu, as tools of western interests – though pointedly, these campaigners themselves were for the most part, based in the West. Cuba's extensive biotechnology business is constrained because – already subject to US embargo – it is too dependent on European custom to put is GM advances into mainstream production.

Though one might have thought that environmentalists would support the turn to a renewable energy source, they are currently engaged in an extensive campaign against the adoption of biofuels in the developing world. It is claimed that these are taking land earmarked for food crops – though these same campaigners have supported the formation of National Parks on 12.65 per cent of the Earth's surface. And of course food crops could easily make way for biofuel production if they were farmed more intensively.

---

[124] 'Biotechnology in Africa', Dr Florence Wambugu, 26 March 2003, http://www.bio.org/foodag/action/20030326.asp, viewed on 14 December 2007
[125] Paul Driessen, *Eco-Imperialism,* Washington, Merril Press, 2004, p. 45

Still, the underlying message is clear. The image of the poor South that the environmentalists prefer is one that is engaged in subsistence farming, not agri-business. Of course, this is a preoccupation that coincides usefully with a growing fear of competition from the developing South in the developed North. In Brazil, sugar-derived ethanol is being farmed as a cheap alternative to petrol, much to the horror of environmentalists. At the same time as the developing world is straining against protectionist measures by European and American farmers, the green lobby is on hand to prevent Asian and African farmers from diversifying into this new growth area.[126]

---

[126] 'US, EU block Brazilian attempt to slash biofuel tariffs at WTO', *International Herald Tribune* November 5, 2007

Indigenism

'The Indian is in no way inferior to the mestizo in his abilities to assimilate progressive techniques of modern production.' Jose Carlos Mariategui[127]

Green imperialists have always felt a bit embarrassed dictating terms to the developing world. Saving the planet so often seemed to mean trashing the poor. Environmentalists needed their own mascots to front up their campaign against industry in the poor South. The greens' preferred object of sympathy was the indigenous people.

In the 1970s the organisation Survival International raised the case of indigenous peoples. In the middle-brow documentary series, *Disappearing World,* embattled indigenous tribesmen were showcased alongside endangered animal species. What was at first a Hampstead taste for peasant knitting got more mainstream as advertisers celebrated the ancient wisdom of aboriginals in the 1990s. A taste for all things indigenous culminated in the United Nations' Decade of the World's Indigenous Peoples (1995–2005), which followed the UN Year of the Indigenous Peoples in 1993.

Hymning the merits of indigenous people also meant making a virtue out of the very low levels of technology they used. Hunter-gathering societies, it was argued were more at peace with the world. Greens embraced the (apocryphal) Australian aboriginal ideal of 'walking on the earth with a light footprint', or Chief Seattle's claim that 'Every part of the earth is sacred to my people'.[128] Anthropologist Marshall Sahlins argued – counter-intuitively – that the world of the hunter-gatherers was a lot more leisurely.[129] Aid programmes favoured

---

[127] Jose Carlos Mariategui, *The Heroic and Creative Meaning of Socialism,* Humanities Press, NJ, 1996, p. 98

[128] In fact the speech was written by screenwriter Ted Perry in 1971, Ron Arnold, *Trashing the Economy,* Washington, Merril Press, 1994, p 39

[129] Marshall Sahlins, *Stone Age Economics.* Hawthorne, Aldine de Gruyter, 1972. Sahlins got his result by changing definitions, assuming that the hunter-gatherers

Heartfield *Green Capitalism*

indigenous technologies and 'indigenous knowledge' over industry and literacy programmes. At last the environmentalists had a Third World champion that did not want a job in town and a car.

The United Nations general secretary named Nobel Prize winner Rigoberta Menchu, a Mayan native of Guatemala, as envoy. Menchu was made a Nobel laureate for raising awareness of indigenous suffering in her harrowing book, *I, Rigoberta Menchu,* which was edited by French radical Elizabeth Burgos-Debray. Menchu's story of the repression of Mayan people won an impassioned hearing in the West, but the UN reforms that she fronted in Guatemala – which would have entrenched the special rights of indigenous people in the constitution – were rejected in a referendum in May 1999. The voters of Guatemala City, who were more likely to be of European descent, in particular saw the reforms as threatening a Balkanization of their country.[130]

David Stoll, an American academic who challenged the veracity of Menchu's account, took issue with the romanticization of indigenous resistance: 'Such works provide rebels in far-off places, into whom careerists can project their fantasies of rebellion'.[131] When I asked Menchu whether she really thought that indigenous peoples were better off without western technology, she replied that, on the contrary, the best solution was democracy and electric pylons – at least that was how V.I. Lenin's slogan 'socialism is soviet power plus electrification' was translated for her.

Environmentalists enjoy the kudos of being champions of the 'first peoples'. But championing the rights of aboriginal people has long been an imperialist strategy. The Aborigines' Protection Society (APS) was founded in 1837 out of a distaste among conservative London society for the rapacious settlers in the colonies – particularly Australia, but also New Zealand, Africa, Fiji, and always with the disaster of

---

experienced no distinction between work and leisure, and so could enjoy their time much more. It would be truer to say that their lives were mostly drudgery.

[130] Alfonso Anzueto, 'Guatemalans count votes on charter changes', *Washington Post,* 17 May. 1999

[131] David Stoll, *Rigoberta Menchu and the Story of all Poor Guatemalans,* Boulder, Westview Press, 1999

American independence in mind. The APS worried about the fate of the savage, disappearing in the spread of civilisation.[132] Though its supporters, often Quakers, were genuinely concerned with the lot of subject peoples, their sympathy did not extend to recognising political rights,[133] but stopped instead at the formation of 'Native Self Government', Chiefs' Councils and so on, as an administrative extension of the Colonial Office.[134] In practice this often meant subordinating the rights of ordinary natives while aggrandising nominated 'Chieftains' in supposedly traditional structures.[135]

The policy of promoting traditional native self government *as an alternative* to political independence was more obviously a hoax in the 1960s and 70s when third world nations were fighting to be free. Few radicals would have taken seriously Rhodesian leader Ian Smith's insistence that the Great Council of Chiefs should take precedence over elected leaders.[136] Most could see through the US administration's sudden interest in the rights of the Miskito Indians in Nicaragua in the 1980s, or the late promotion of the rights of Zulu chief Gatsha Buthelezi as being little more than an attempt to stop the African National Congress taking power in South Africa. But today, when the clamour for independence is not so great, it is easier to let the image of the downtrodden indigenous people supplant the actual state of the industrious labourers of the developing world.

The *reductio ad absurdum* of indigenism came in the Philippines in June, 1971. The Minister for Tribal Minorities Manda Elizalde announced the discovery of a stone-age tribe, lauded in *National Geographic* and in a coffee table anthropology book by John Nance *The Gentle Tasaday* . President Marcos passed a decree that these Ur-folk should be protected from all outside contact, though his

---

[132] Jacob Gruber, 'Ethnographic Salvage and the Shaping of Anthropology', *American Anthropologist,* Vol 72, no. 6, 1970, 1294

[133] Kenneth Nworah, 'The Aborigines Protection Society', *Canadian Journal of African Studies,* Vol. 5, No.1 86

[134] See Suke Wolton, *Lord Hailey, the Colonial Office and the Politics of Race and Empire in the Second World War,* London, Macmillan, 2000

[135] See Peter France, *The Charter of the Land,* Melbourne, Oxford University Press, 1969

[136] Ian Smith, *The Great Betrayal,* London, Blake Publishing, 1997, p.81-2

wife helicoptered celebrities like Gina Lollobrigida and Charles Lindbergh for special visits. Of course the Tasaday were not a stone age tribe at all, but just impoverished T'Boli people, who had so few tools and modern goods that they looked like cave-dwellers. The Marcos clan had used the 'Tasaday' to weave a myth about the Philippines' origins, and kept these unfortunates in poverty so that they could be the totem in that myth.[137]

The emotional weight of pro-indigenist campaigns added a new dimension to the anti-globalization movement. Environmental organizations which were active against large-scale development projects had been open to the charge that they were the voice of the developed world, withholding further development from the less developed. But now, by taking up the cause of indigenous peoples, they substituted a romantic alternative to development-oriented Third World nationalism. The indigenous peoples themselves, as largely ill-organized populations who were unlikely to benefit from economic growth, were the ideal foil for the environmentalists.

On a practical level, the indigenist campaigns had a more specific purpose. Indigenous land claims were more likely to be granted when public authorities were seeking to withdraw farmland from production. On 18 October 1983, Ronald Reagan surprised his critics by signing over 1250 acres of land to the Mashantucket Pequod that had been sold to farmers by the State of Connecticut in 1856. But then Reagan's administration was already struggling with the problem of retiring farmland, and honouring native land rights was as good an excuse to put the produce of these fields outside of the mainstream agricultural market. Back in 1938 Roosevelt had done a similar thing, signing over tens of thousands of acres to the Seminoles – just after an intense agricultural crisis of 'overproduction' had been forcibly resolved by taking great swathes of US farmland out of service. In Latin America governments have granted indigenous land rights to prevent the spread of land-squatting by peasants. The indigenous land claims are easier to deal with – because they are strictly limited in their scope – than the spontaneous movement of landless peasants. Denying them

---

[137] James Hamilton Paterson, *America's Boy,* London, Granta, 1999, p. 351-3

land in the name of indigenism is the means to make them into propertyless wage slaves.

Green Colonialism

The natural trajectory of environmental protection towards the developing world is for the concerned North to assume direct territorial control. Johan Eliasch is a banker, film producer, chief executive of the Head Sportswear company, deputy treasurer of the Conservative Party and now advisor to Prime Minister Gordon Brown. In 2006, Eliasch, whose fortune is estimated at £335 million, also became proud owner of a 400,000 acre plot in the heart of the Amazon rain forest, bought from a logging company. Eliasch's sole interest in the land is to withhold it from Brazilians who would want to develop it. 'The Amazon is the lung of the world' says Eliasch, who is very excited about the bio-diversity on his new Brazilian estate, which is rich in dolphins, piranha fish and marmosets. Eliasch also supports a charity, Cool Earth, which buys up the Amazon forest on behalf of Western patrons. So far Cool Earth has bought some £32,000 worth in Brazil and Ecuador, charging its patrons £72 an acre. In America, Calor Gas heir Paul van Vlissingen is spending £15 million of his billion pound fortune buying land for nature parks in four African countries.[138]

Not everyone appreciates Eliasch's benevolent imperialism. Indigenous leader Davi Kopenawa Yanomami, claims Eliasch has exaggerated the benefits of his 'useless' scheme:

> You napëpë [whites],want to buy pieces of rainforest. This is useless. The forest cannot be bought; it is our life and we have always protected it. Give us back our lands and our health before it's too late for us and for you.[139]

---

[138] *Sunday Times,* 19 March 2006
[139] *Independent,* 10 October 2007, http://news.independent.co.uk/people/pandora/article3043746.ece, viewed on 14 December 2004

8. ENVIRONMENTALISTS IN THE 'DISMAL SCIENCE'

Latter-day environmentalists are irritated with economics. They object to the cost-benefit analyses that do not account for nature. They attack the 'Washington Consensus' of free market economists working at the World Bank and the International Monetary fund. The Washington Consensus, according to today's environmentalists is making a fetish out of runaway growth that is trashing the environment.

But mainstream economics (sometimes called 'neo-classical' economics, for its return to the ideas of Adam Smith) is not really growth-oriented. Like environmentalism, neo-classical economics takes scarcity as a given. According to Lionel Robbins' much-lauded account 'Economics is the science which studies human behaviour as a relationship between ends and scarce means which have alternative uses.'[140]

Neo-classical economics is interested first and foremost in *equilibrium* or balance. The central claim of neo-classical economics is that the unimpeded market is a self-equilibriating system. Prices carry information that allows the equilibrium to reassert itself. Where supply is too great in relation to demand, prices fall, and producers reduce output; where supply is to small, prices will rise and producers increase output. Any disturbances or disproportionalities are quickly overcome as long as markets are free, according to the theory.

Taking equilibrium as its essential grounding, neo-classical economics has no room for growth in its theory. Growth is an external factor to neo-classical economics.[141] The nearest thing to growth in the neo-classical theory is the welfare gains that come with the optimum distribution of goods. Production remains a technical factor external to

---

[140] Lionel Robbins, *An Essay on the Nature and Significance of Economic Science*, London, Macmillan, 1945, p. 16

[141] Economic theories of growth were awkwardly grafted onto neo-classical economic theory, by J.M. Keynes, W.W. Rostow and John Hicks – usually in a defensive reaction to the rise of the Socialist and Third World nationalist movements.

the subject of economics proper, market exchanges. Productivity growth is fundamentally a disturbance to the market equilibrium.

Though the greens have forgotten today, ecological theory was largely cribbed from economic theories of equilibrium. The word ecology was popularised by the now-discredited biologist Ernst Haekel (1834-1919), who thought that all nature was united in one self-correcting system, and that even politics was 'applied biology'. In the nineteenth century defenders of the status quo insisted that the distribution of property between rich and poor was a law of nature that could not be broken. In books like *Social Statics* and *Physics and Politics* ('the application of the principles of natural selection and inheritance to political society',) Herbert Spencer and Walter Bagehot made the case for what they called 'Social Darwinism'.

The economists' belief that social stratification was ordained by nature mirrored the early ecologists' belief that nature itself was in a state of equilibrium. Elaborating on geologist Eduard Suess's demarcation of a 'biosphere' and Arthur Roy Harrod's ecosystem, ecologists like Arthur Tansley argued that 'mature well-integrated plant communities had enough of the characters of organisms to be considered as quasi-organisms'.[142] In 1979 James Lovelock took the argument one stage further, saying that the role that organic life played in sustaining the atmosphere indicated all the features of intelligence. Lovelock called this intelligence *Gaia,* after the Greek goddess of life. But Lovelock was making use of a poor definition of intelligent life as self-correcting feedback mechanisms, taken from cyberneticist Norbert Wiener theory of artificial intelligence. In truth such self-correcting mechanisms, as most biologists agreed, were simply *stochastic,* or chance occurrences.

Pre-modern, holistic ideas of a natural balance, that project an imaginary totality onto manifold nature, are well entrenched in the popular mind. What is more, it is widely assumed that human industry is increasingly out of balance with nature, and even in some quarters that nature's equilibrium will reassert itself in mass human extinction.

---

[142] 'in the same way that human communities are habitually considered so', Arthur Tansley, 'The use and abuse of vegetational concepts and terms', *Ecology,* Vol. 16, No. 3, July 1935, p.290

To some misanthropes, mankind is even seen as a human plague.[143] More acceptably, it is common to treat the interchange between man and nature as if it were a market exchange, subject to the laws of equilibrium. So eco-spokesman Michael Jacob suggests that 'the natural environment performs the function of a capital stock for the human economy' as a preamble to the argument that 'economic activity is currently running down this stock'.[144]

Despite past hostilities, ecologists and neo-classical economists are busy re-discovering their common ground. Bank of England economist Sir Nicholas Stern's report on the presumed costs of climate change was a turning point for the suits. Having shed the view of unkempt green slackers, free marketeers like Newt Gingrich and Margaret Thatcher are telling us that they always believed in keeping a proper balance with nature.[145]

And, being essentially systems of rationing, many environmental policies give more than a passing nod to the science of rationing, neo-classical economics. London Mayor Ken Livingstone admitted as much when he conceded that his congestion charge was drawn from an idea of the free market ideologue Milton Friedman. One unique contribution of environmentalism to the 'dismal science' of economics has been in the theories of 'externalities' – which is a fascinating insight into the way that capitalism projects social goals that are increasingly at odds with the outcome of market exchanges – and in that of 'natural capital'.

The theory of Externalities

In the early 1960s the *laissez faire* economist Arthur Seldon persuaded his friend E.J. Mishan to write a book about his doubts on economic growth. *The Costs of Economic Growth* was published in 1967 and

---

[143] See John Gray, *Straw Dogs: thoughts on humans and other animals,* London, Granta, 2003
[144] *The Politics of the Real World,* London, Earthscan, 1996, p.17
[145] See Newt Gingrich, *A Contract with the Earth,* Baltimore, John Hopkins University Press, 2007

immediately became a foundation stone of green economic thinking. Mishan shared Seldon's prejudice in favour of the free market – 'neo-classical economics' – but he despaired at the implications of growth. Not to put too fine a point on it, Mishan despaired at the increased wealth of the working classes. 'Official support for arbitrary growth targets has as much as invited annual wage claims by the trades unions' he moaned. 'Having so assiduously sown the seeds of rising expectations, we are reaping the harvest of rising prices'.[146]

Things that made ordinary people happy only upset the LSE economics professor, as his own income no longer set him quite so high above the college janitor. He warned of 'the postwar surge of affluence in the West, much of it channelled into communications, in particular the mushroom growth of television, automobile ownership, air travel and mass tourism' and of 'the unprecedented expansion of the human species having ecological consequences we are only beginning to perceive'.[147]

Today, when environmentalists like to think of their movement as part of the opposition to free market thinking. But as we have seen modern environmentalism came out of capitalist ideas about scarcity. It was a compromise between the hardline free-marketeers and the state-spending Keynesians that growth was ever included in economic theory at all. Looked at closely, neo-classical economics only acknowledges welfare benefits arising out of redistribution, not growth as such. The ascendance of the free market neo-classical economics in the 1970s and 1980s really was a return to the idea that the market was there to distribute limited resources.

Mishan's contribution was to vilify growth in the theory of 'external diseconomies'. The theory did modify the neo-classical theory of prices in one important respect. Neo-classical economists had asserted that prices were a true reflection of people's wants, and so it was wrong to disturb its free operation. What Mishan argued was that not all welfare benefits or dis-benefits were reflected in market prices. There were, as the economists agreed, some benefits that came free of

---

[146] E. J. Mishan, *The Costs of Economic Growth,* Harmondsworth, Penguin, 1979, p. 36

[147] Mishan, *The Costs of Economic Growth,* p. 17

charge, as it were. If your neighbour paid to have his house painted, it also improved the neighbourhood, free of cost. These effects are 'external economies' – 'external' in that they are not represented in the market price.

Mishan drew attention to what he called 'external diseconomies', that is, harms done that are not reflected in the price. So a factory that pays for the raw materials and rent for the land it uses does not pay for the air that it pollutes.

All that Mishan really contributed to economic science was to show that prices did not account for everything (which most people outside the monastic order of neo-classical economics knew anyway). The idea of 'diseconomies' was valuable to defenders of private property because it allowed them to acknowledge what the law had conceded many years before – that industry would have to be fined for damage it did to others. Indeed insofar as Mishan's theory helped people to misrepresent civil liabilities as costs, that is to assimilate law to economics, it introduced an error. The 'polluter pays' principle sounds very militant, but in the end it only means that businesses can buy their way out of responsibility for the harm they do. If expected returns on a new product are great enough, why not factor the risk of compensation claims into the budget, cynical MDs might think?

The theory of 'external diseconomies' (or 'public bads') was elaborated much further. Its meaning was extended without limit to 'prove' that untold harm was being done that we did not even know about. In the estimation of petrol taxes, it was asserted that drivers were, as a group, liable for the additional costs to the NHS of respiratory problems, road accidents and, of course, global warming. Factoring in these fictional 'costs' to the price of petrol was supposed to justify the increased duties.

On this basis policy makers ignored the statistical evidence that in nine out of ten journeys, the public prefer to travel by car than by public transport. The demand for driving, the policy makers insisted, does not reflect its true cost. So more money was raised by taxing motorists, some of it spent on public transport, while road-building was suspended. Municipal authorities (actually realising that cars were very valuable to their owners) charged them to park at their own curbsides, and even for the pleasure of traffic congestion.

Of course, public authorities have every right to tax any person or activity that they decide. What did not make sense was to disguise this public policy as a price, pretending that a government act was really just the true price of driving. It is a sign of the diminished authority of the state that it has to pass its duties off as charges. What is more, the punitive aspect of the policy, never being properly justified before the public, was unrestrained. When the British government's 'fuel duty escalator' got to be too much, fuel protestors paralysed the country, and millions signed a Downing Street web petition against it. Having persuaded themselves that the duty was justified as the true price of petrol, the government were surprised to find that in fact it was just a policy that could be overturned by the public.

The theory of externalities did not only diminish public authority to the level of pricing decisions. It also introduced a corresponding confusion about prices. Prices were thought to be spontaneous. But the theory of externalities suggested that prices could be set to accommodate public goods. In truth, these are not prices at all, but legally enforced taxes. The confusion indicates the way that the long-term interests of the capitalist system might deviate from the day-to-day operation of the market. To maintain the health of the private property system overall, the specific rights of private property could be modified.

In this way the theory of externalities amends neoclassical economic theory to bring it into line with the new green capitalism. The ordinary operation of the market rewards producers who meet customers' wants tending towards more goods at cheaper prices – in a word, plenty. But under the theory of externalities artificial scarcities can be created by factoring in notional and open-ended 'social costs'.

The non-rational character of the theory is betrayed when only diseconomies are taken into account. What about the positive external economies – those uncosted benefits of industrial progress. In the case of petrol, the positive impact of mobility, the way that it adds to the gregariousness and cosmopolitanism of modern life would be difficult to quantify. And what of the 3.8 million emergencies attended by the ambulance services each year in the UK, or half million fires attended? The cost of the 4.5 million tons of freight carried each day on our roads are reflected in their price at the supermarket, but not the positive acculturation of society generally that arises from their consumption. That these external benefits are ignored, while the problems are inflated shows that the theory of externalities is at heart an intuitive, non-rational and one-sided protest against modern industry.

> 'Cheap air travel is great for our civilisation', EU Commission President Jose Manuel Barroso[148]

In 1615 Galileo Galilei wrote his *Considerations on the Copernican System*, weighing the merits of the Ptolemaic (rotating around the earth) and Copernican (rotating around the Sun) theories of the universe. One fact that pulled in Copernicus' favour were the endlessly complicated 'epicycles' that Ptolemy's theory needed to 'save the appearances'. Epicycles were additional rotations added to the astrolabe to make the model fit with the observed movements of the planets. Galileo saw that many of these weird movements fell away if you started with planets moving around the sun.

E.J. Mishan's theory attempts to bang more and more data into the theory of market prices. But this data just does not fit except by twisting the meaning of basic economic terms – 'price', 'cost' and so on – beyond recognition. Rather than try to 'save the appearances', by endlessly tweaking the theory in this artificial way, we should ask why the theory of the market does not correspond to reality.[149]

Today's green capitalists are often found making money not out of tangible goods, but legal titles: carbon rights, planning gain, carbon offsets and so on. E.J. Mishan's theory of externalities gives a justification for the legal titles that substitute for tangible goods. It is a conceptualisation of a claim on society's surplus wealth that is

---

[148] *Independent*, 23 March 2007

[149] A fascinating paper by Daniel Lloyd for the CBI shows just how far legislation qualifying consumer sovereignty and the finality of contract law has gone, suggesting that the courts already think that market exchange is a poor approximation of contemporary social relations, 'Paper on Consumer Regulation, Blue Skies Project'.

independent of the production process... or even comes about by setting limits on industry. Properly named the theory of externalities it indicates that green capitalists expect returns *external* from the process of capitalist production.

One of those that elaborated Mishan's theory of externalities was Charles Pearce (1941-2005). Taking advantage of 'the abrupt conversion of the Thatcher government to environmentalism in the late 1980s', Pearce injected an environmental dimension into the free-market world of Conservative economic policy'.[150]

Pearce's method was to stretch the meaning of economic categories to cover phenomena broader than market exchanges. In that way the world's natural resources could be labelled 'natural capital'. In the stroke of a pen, as it were, Pearce laid claim to ownership of natural resources across the globe, in the name of future generations. Of course these were not property rights in any real sense, but political claims to rights of control, even extra-territorial control, over resources belonging to others, or just unclaimed. Like the theory of 'externalities', natural capital was a usefully imprecise notion that could be filled with whatever content was convenient to policy-makers.

---

[150] Obiturary, Stephen Smith, *Guardian,* 22 September 2005

9. GREEN SOCIALISM? NO THANKS

'Our demands most moderate are, we only want the Earth.' James Connolly, 1907

No doubt many greens would be just as critical of the hypocrisies of green capitalism. Some would say that there is another kind of environmentalism, one that is not about making money. Green socialism might look like a better choice than green capitalism. But it is not.

Since the decline of Social Democracy in Europe, and of Stalinism in the east, there have been a number of attempts to revive the fortunes of the left by associating with environmentalism. That project is bound to fail if, as argued here, environmentalism is at heart the ideology of capitalism in its retreat from production.

Austerity Socialism

Modern green thinking owes a lot of its ideas to the tradition of *austerity socialism.* From the outset, romantic anti-capitalists had an influence on the socialist tradition. The high Tory John Ruskin's *Unto This Last,* a protest against modern industry on the part of the dignity of craft labour, was influential. Ruskin's follower William Morris moved gradually from romantic anti-capitalism to a more forward-looking socialism.

When working class representation led to the election of socialists to office in Europe they were often confronted with the dilemma of administrating capitalist societies. And since their election was, by and large, the consequence of popular discontent during times of economic recession, they were often in office just when the tough cut-backs in jobs and welfare had to be seen through.

These office-bound socialists owed their influence to a promise that they could persuade working people to accept cuts in their living standards, as long as they were 'socialist cuts'. Austerity socialism was the political programme of the Socialist governments of the inter-war period, and of post war rationing in Britain. Labour's participation in the national government during the war, and its experience of administrating rationing was formative. Memories of the Second World War had featured in the Labour Party's appeal to the electorate in the 1983 election as 'our 1945 victory' when 'we set to work creating a real community'.[151]

The British Labour Party claimed to be the natural party of government in the late sixties and seventies on the grounds that only it could deliver the cuts that capitalism needed to survive – 'proud of the contribution we made to the nation's salvation at critical times in our history, and it is in that same spirit that we approach the interlocking crises of the 1970s'.[152] Labour introduced the 'Social Contract' – compulsory pay restraint, or what Harold Wilson called 'the fair sharing of the sacrifice'.[153] Labour promoted austerity in the name of a fair distribution of what little there was. Redistributing the misery was the meaning of austerity socialism, and its common cause with environmentalism today.

Green Socialism

Environmentalists have drawn upon the tradition of socialist austerity. They see their own hostility to mass consumption mirrored in the socialist case for cutting back. Writer Madeleine Bunting and the New Economics Foundation's Andrew Simm have both called for a return to wartime rationing to beat climate change. Fabian Society chair Michael Jacobs summed up the argument in the 1996 election commentary *The*

---

[151] Michael Foot, foreword, *The New Hope for Britain,* London, The Labour Party, 1983, p. 5
[152] *Let Us Work Together – Labour's Way Out of the Crisis,* London, Labour Party, 1974, p 1
[153] *The Times,* 29 November 1974, p 8

Politics of the Real World: 'it cannot therefore be expected that the disposable incomes of ordinary, reasonably comfortable households in Britain will rise significantly year on year as the political system has come to expect'.[154]

Green Marxism?

In direct contrast to the austerity socialism of the reformist leaders is the cornucopian socialism of Karl Marx, Frederick Engels, V.I. Lenin and Leon Trotsky. These more militant socialists were not interested in half a loaf, but wanted the bakery. Austerity to them was a mean, disfiguring condition that had to be abolished.

Recent books by John Bellamy Foster and Paul Burkett have tried to unearth a 'Green Marx', largely elaborated from his few asides about soil erosion, and some speculative elaboration of Engels' theory of a Dialectics of Nature.[155] The 'Green Marx' is a wilful misreading of Marx's work, which is plainly a 'productivist' criticism of the narrow parsimony of capitalism.

In Marx's theory, the development of the productive forces is the means by which the realm of human freedom is enlarged, as the realm of necessity, of human labour is reduced to a minimum. In the rough draft for *Capital,* the *Grundrisse,* Marx wrote:

> Real economy – saving – consists of the saving of labour time (minimum (and minimisation) of production costs); but this saving identical with development of productive force. Hence in no way abstinence from consumption, but rather the development of the power, of capabilities of production, and hence of the capabilities as well as the means of consumption.[156]

---

[154] Michael Jacobs, *The Politics of the Real World,* London, Earthscan, 1996, p. 35
[155] See Jean-Paul Sartre, *Critique of Dialectical Reason,* London, Verso, 1991, p. 27-8
[156] Karl Marx, *Grundrisse,* Harmondsworth, Penguin, 1973, p. 711

In *Capital,* Marx is scathing about the barriers to mechanisation that arise from Capital's undervaluation of labour power. He points out that as long as labour is paid less than the value it creates that will make the introduction of technology less attractive than the use of cheap labour. 'Hence nowhere do we find a more shameful squandering of human labour-power for the most despicable purposes that in England, the land of machinery'.[157]

And in the penultimate chapter Marx reprises the formulations of the 1848 *Communist Manifesto,* which Bellamy Foster and Paul Burkett dismiss as youthful excess, again celebrating the liberating power of industry:

> The monopoly of capital becomes a fetter upon the mode of production, which has sprung up and flourished along with and under it. Centralisation of the means of production and socialisation of labour at last reach a point where they become incompatible with their capitalist integument. Thus integument is burst asunder.[158]

Marx continues in this vein in third volume *Capital.* In a discussion of economist David Ricardo and the tendency of the rate of profit to fall, he makes this telling point:

> Development of the productive forces of social labour is the historical task and justification of capital. This is just the way that it unconsciously creates the material requirements of a higher mode of production.[159]

Marx continues that the falling rate of profit is only an indicator that capitalist social relations are historically redundant *because* they have become a barrier to the further development of social productivity.

---

[157] Karl Marx, *Capital,* Vol. I, Moscow, Progress, 1974, p. 372
[158] Karl Marx, *Capital,* p. 715
[159] Karl Marx, *Capital,* Vol. III, 1959, p. 259

> It comes to the surface here in a purely economic way – i.e. from the bourgeois point of view ... – that it has its barrier, that it [Capital] is relative, that it is not an absolute, but only a historical mode of production corresponding to a definite limited epoch in the development of the material requirements of production. [160]

Marx was, far from being a proto-environmentalist, very much a Victorian champion of industrial progress – albeit one who saw private property as ultimately a barrier to further development. He scorned the environmentalists of his own day. This was what Marx had to say against the 'true socialist' doctrine of a harmony between man and nature proposed by Daumer:

> We see here that the superficiality and ignorance of the speculating founder of a new religion is transformed into very pronounced cowardice. Herr Daumer flees the historic tragedy that is threatening him too closely to alleged nature, i.e. to mere rustic idyll, and preaches the cult of the female to cloak his own effeminate resignation.
> ...
>
> We see that this cult of nature is limited to Sunday walks of an inhabitant of a small provincial town who childishly wonders at the cuckoo laying its eggs in another bird's nest, at tears being designed to keep the surface of the eyes moist, and so on. There is no question, of course of modern sciences, which, with modern industry, have revolutionised the whole of nature and put an end to man's childish attitude to nature as well as to other forms of childishness ... For the rest it would be desirable that Bavaria's sluggish peasant economy, the ground on which priests and Daumers likewise grow, should at last be ploughed up by modern cultivation and modern machines. [161]

---

[160] Marx, *Capital,* Vol. III, p. 259
[161] Quoted in Alfred Schmidt, *The Concept of nature in Marx,* London, Verso, p. 131-3

Marx's students were just as emphatic in their rejection of the doom-mongering views that would later be made by the environmentalists. Trotsky wrote:

> Marxism sets out from the development of technique as the fundamental spring of progress, and constructs the communist programme upon the dynamics of the productive forces. If you conceive that some cosmic catastrophe is going to destroy our planet in the fairly near future, then you must, of course, reject the communist perspective along with much else. Except for this as yet problematic danger, however, there is not the slightest scientific ground for setting any limit in advance to our technical productive and cultural possibilities. Marxism is saturated with the optimism of progress.[162]

In *The Permanent Revolution* (1930) Trotsky argued, 'industrialization is the driving force of the whole of modern culture and by this token the *only* conceivable basis for socialism'.[163]

While greens demand restrictions on consumption Trotsky looked forward to cornucopia. In *If America Should Go Communist* (1934), for example, Trotsky argues that under Communism 'control over individual consumption – whether by money or administration – will no longer be necessary when there is more than enough of everything for everybody'.[164]

---

[162] Leon Trotsky, *The Revolution Betrayed,* New York, Pathfinder Press, 1972, p. 45; and see Sandy Irvine, 'The Prophet Misarmed: Trotsky, Ecology and Sustainability', *What Next?* 31, 2007, for an ecologist's critique

[163] Leon Trotsky, *Permanent Revolution,* Introduction to the German edition, http://www.marxists.org/archive/trotsky/1931/tpr/prge.htm, viewed on 14 December 2007

[164] Leon Trotsky, *If America Should Go Communist,* 1934, http://www.marxists.org/archive/trotsky/1934/08/ame.htm, viewed on 14 December 2007

10 THE UNNATURAL LIMITS TO GROWTH

Can capitalism really go green? It already has. Environmentalists say the adoption of green charters by big business is so much greenwashing. They are just holding out for more say in what business does, and for a bigger reward for their services.

Can green strategies work for big business? There will always be problems. Capitalism is a system that relies upon growth, as well as constraint. The green agenda only emphasizes one aspect. There will always be a clash between the capitalist instinct to produce more goods, and its narrower goal of making profits. Using green business strategies to engineer scarcity is not a long-term strategy for success, it is a means to sustain profitability in the here and now.

Engineering land scarcity had the effect of pushing up farm prices. In 2007 British supermarkets Asda and Sainsburys were fined for colluding to keep milk, cheese and butter prices high. They claim that they intended to pass on the £270m mark-up to farmers – though somehow it never got to them. The supermarkets were caught out, but the strategy of creating scarcity by land retirement is the bigger fix. It has pushed food prices up by three quarters since 2005.

Setting caps on energy production, industrial output, car transport and house-building in the name of saving the environment all have the effect of damaging people's standard of living. But as we have seen, that does not stop individual businesses from making big profits out of those caps. Trading in carbon rights, making windmills, carbon offsetting schemes, and organic food are all ways of making profits out of artificial limits set upon growth.

In 2008, though, the effect of green strategies for limiting growth is having an impact on the economy overall. Nobody needs to be surprised that economic growth has been undermined. That is the explicit strategy of green capitalism.

Green critics like to argue that the current credit crunch is caused by consumerist excess. Too much buying on credit has led to the problems in the economy. Of course it is true that consumers have been relying too much on credit. But the extraordinary price rises in the housing market are not only down to easy credit, but also to restrictions on housebuilding. US and European dependence upon East Asian manufacturing has come about because of low growth rates in the West – and these are bound up with adoption of anti-growth business strategies. Western economies are dependent on future earnings to meet consumer demands in the here and now because they are failing to innovate.

The fear of 'excessive' economic expansion led central banks to raise interest rates, choking off consumer demand – as well as exposing the bad debt that banks and building societies were holding. The credit crunch itself would be readily offset if Western economies were working at full capacity, rather than shackled by low growth business strategies and economic policies.

Having called for constraints on growth, environmentalists ought to own up that recession was exactly what they were after. The limits on consumer spending, the slowing job growth, the fall in inventories are just what they counselled as the strategy of green capitalism. The rising energy costs, house repossessions and food prices are the condition of 'green growth'. These are the unnatural limits that green capitalists put upon growth, the better to wring profits out of scarcity.

But it is unlikely that green capitalism will get the blame for the current economic difficulties. The green bandwagon will not be so easily overturned. More likely is that the finger of blame will be pointed once again at ordinary consumers, for their supposed excess and 'unrealistic' expectations. Having damaged the economy overall for their own sectional advantage, the green capitalists will turn the problem into an argument for more green policies. For the rest of us, it is green capitalism that is unrealistic, and an unnatural limit upon the world of plenty that is all around us, waiting to be realised.

APPENDIX:
THE REVOLUTION IN TECHNIQUE

The Factory

Half a million people work in 52 'economic zones' in the Philippines, like the Cavite Export Processing Zone, in Rosario, where Nike Running shoes, Gap pyjamas, IBM computer screens and Old Navy jeans tumble off the production line.[165] In the Samyang factory 32 km west of Ho Chi Minh City 5200 people, mostly young women, make 600,000 Nike shoes a month.[166] In the Suame Magazine, Ghana, 40,000 live and work in the complex of car repair workshops and allied trades.[167] Since it was opened in 1997, the Daventry International Rail Freight Terminal Logistics Park has expanded to cover 23 million square feet of warehouses and factories. Every year 1.2 million American Wal-Mart employees shelve and ring out the contents the half a million containers shipped from overseas.[168]

Modern industry is built on the factory system. Before the coming of the factory, industry took place in the home. But this cottage industry struggled to keep up with demand once merchants bought up their goods for sale. John and Thomas Lombe built the first factory to throw silk in 1721. 150 metres long, it housed 300 workers, on an island in the Derwent.[169] Fifty years later, in nearby Cromford, Richard Arkwright built the first of many cotton mills, where 5000 people worked. Around the same time Josiah Wedgwood opened his Etruria Works making pottery, and Abraham Darby II began production of steel rails at his works in Coalbrookdale. Between 1838 and 1861 the

---

[165] Klein, *No Logo,* London, Flamingo, 2000, p. 203
[166] Legrain, *Open World,* London, Abacus, 2002, p. 55
[167] David Edgerton, *The Shock of the Old,* London, Profile, 2006, p. 83
[168] mostly China, Moira Herbst, *Labor Research* 5 July 2005; Edgerton, *The Shock of the Old,* p. 74
[169] Philip Sauvain, *British Economic and Social History,* Cheltenham, Stanley Thornes, 1987, p. 51

number of cotton workers grew from 250,000 to 500,000 - by which time one million Britons were in manufacturing.

Cotton and Calico mills employing thousands were opened in Chemnitz early in the nineteenth century, along with Silk and Cotton mills in the Rhineland.[170] After a long period of stagnation, German industry emulated British growth at the end of the nineteenth century with new businesses like electricity, where Siemens and AEG employed 129,000, and Bayer and Hoechst's chemical businesses.

In the USA, in 1851 Cyrus McCormick opened his Chicago reaper works with 33 employees.[171] In 1858 I.M Singer opened his sewing machine factory in Mott Street, New York, and by 1865 1,100 were working there and at another site on Delancey Street.[172] In 1903 the Henry Ford Motor Company opened in Detroit and in 1908 made the first 'Model-T' mass-produced car.

With economies of scale, the elimination of waste, pooled resources and a rational division of labour, the factory system boosted output massively, as can be seen in the way that the industrialised nations left the others behind. In India, handloom weavers were put out of work by English Cotton mills, who increased their exports there from one million yards in 1814 to one billion in 1870.[173]

In time of course, the factory system was copied across the world. In Russia the number of factories rose from 2400 to 15,000 between 1804 and 1860;[174] by 1914 there were two million industrial workers, nearly half of which were in factories with more than a thousand employees.[175]

---

[170] Franz Mehring, *Absolutism and Revolution in Germany,* London, 1975, New Park, 163-4

[171] David Hounshell, *From the American System to Mass Production,* Baltimore, John Hopkins UP, 1984, p. 157

[172] Hounshell, *From the American System to Mass Production,* p 93; by 1905 Singer's factories employed 30,000 worldwide, Edgerton, *The Shock of the Old,* p. 58

[173] Paul Kennedy, *The Rise and Fall of the Great Powers,* London, Fontana, 1990, p.191

[174] Kennedy, *The Rise and Fall of the Great Powers,* p. 219

[175] Leon Trotsky, *The History of the Russian Revolution,* London, Pluto, 1985, p. 32, 55

Relative share of world manufacturing output 1750-1900, per cent,

	1750	1800	1830	1860	1880	1900
Europe	23.2	28.1	34.2	53.2	61.3	62
Britain	1.9	4.3	9.5	19.9	22.9	18.5
Germany	2.9	3.5	3.5	4.9	8.5	13.2
USA	0.1	0.8	2.4	7.2	14.7	23.6
Third World	73	67.7	60.5	36.6	20.9	11

Kennedy, *Rise and Fall of the Great Powers*, p. 190

In China 78 new cotton mills were opened between 1916 and 1923, 178 new cigarette factories between 1915 and 1927.[176] In Japan, the state organised heavy industry while smaller textile factories grew up in the early twentieth century.[177] After the Second World War, the expansion of industry was interrupted by the repatriation of capital to fund European reconstruction. Most of the non-western world stagnated, with the exception of Japan and Korea. But since the 1970s the factory system has exploded again, across, the 'Asian Tiger' economies in the 1980s (Malaysia, Taiwan) and through China and Vietnam in the 1990s.

Machinery

Putting craftsmen under the same roof changed the way they work, first because it made the division of labour - the proportions in which labourers had to be distributed in different activities - transparent, and more easily organised. Over and above that, though, the factory system led to a revolution in the production process. Tools were augmented by machines. Machines - frames, jibs, trolleys and other mechanical

---

[176] Harold Isaacs, *The Tragedy of the Chinese Revolution*, Stanford UP, 1961, p. 21
[177] Jon Halliday, *A Political History of Japanese Capitalism*, New York, Monthly Review Press, 1975, p. 59

devices - held the tools.[178] Mechanisation let workers hold more tools than they had hands, and so make more goods in the same amount of time. Machines supplemented muscle power with levers and wheels, and invited the use of non-human energy. They led to more uniformly made goods. And they made workers - often called 'hands' - interchangeable as the plan of work resided in the machine settings more than in the craftsman's skills.

James Hargreaves' Spinning Jenny (1764), a frame that ran eight spindles off one wheel increased cotton yarn output (which was struggling to keep up with weavers using John Kay's 'flying shuttle' since 1733). Richard Arkwright improved on the Jenny with his Spinning Frame using paired rollers (1762), and Samuel Crompton combined elements of both in his 'Mule' (1779). In 1787 Edmund Cartwright mechanised cotton weaving with his 'power loom'. The mechanisation of cotton was the model for mass production from bottles to cars. In 1798, the British Navy built a block making plant at Portsmouth (a ship block is the wooden block that tightens rigging) and four years later Mark Isambard Brunel perfected a mechanised block-making process. In 1913 The Ford Motor Company introduced the first moving assembly line, to put together magnetos, having previously moved teams around static cars on stands.[179]

Engineering

Once production was mechanised, the impetus was to substitute muscle-power with non-human energy. Arkwright's Spinning Frame was too heavy to be worked by hand and depended on a water wheel; Cartwright's power loom used steam power, as did Brunel's block-making plant. Newcomen made a pump powered by steam pressure in 1712. At Boulton's works in 1765 James Watt made it faster with the addition of a separate condensing chamber, added a fly-wheel, throttle and governor to make it an engine turning a wheel. Then in 1801

---

[178] Karl Marx, *Capital,* Vol. I, Moscow, Progress, 1974, p. 353
[179] Hounshell, *From the American System to Mass Production,* p. 246

Richard Trevithick dispensed with the condensing chamber by delivering steam to the cylinder under pressure. Compound engines developed in the 1850s used the same steam twice over, first to drive one piston then another. In 1894 the Anglo-Irish aristocrat Charles Algernon Parsons patented a steam turbine which could drive a propeller.[180]

In 1867 Henry Wilde, building on Faraday's discoveries on electromagnetism, generated electricity from motion to make the first dynamo, which was used to make silver plating. Belgian Zenobé Gramme reversed the operation of a dynamo to make the first electric motor in 1873; the former Edison engineer Nikola Tesla's 1882 motor using alternating current is in essence the one in your washing machine. Water, wind or steam powered machinery depended on complicated belts and chains to distribute motive power through the factory, but electric motors could be powered by cable.

In 1866 Nicolaus Otto built a two-stroke, gas powered internal combustion engine (igniting fuel in the cylinder to drive the wheel) in Cologne, and ten years later a horizontal four-stroke compression engine. In 1886 the first gasoline-powered internal combustion engines were made in Germany.[181] In 1893 Rudolf Diesel patented the engine that carries his name - which ignited fuel in the cylinder by pressure, rather than a spark. In 1930 Frank Whittle patented the Jet engine which drew in air burned it with fuel spewing exhaust gases out the back, by which displacement the whole thing is thrown forward at fantastic speeds - an example of moving from a batch process (the internal combustion engine) to a continuous one (the jet engine). Like Ford's continuous production lines, they are usually harder difficult, but more effective.

Henry Maudslay's engineering works founded in London in 1791 developed the first standardised screws for bolts, as well as developing a slide rest for lathes and the first micrometer. Precision engineering allowed much greater machine and engine efficiency, just as standardisation of parts speeded the production process.

---

[180] Geoffrey Blainey, *The Tyranny of Distance,* Sydney, Macmillan, 2001, p.271
[181] Vaclav Smil, *Energy,* Oxford, One World, 2006, p. 104

Energy

Energy usually means heat, light or kinetic energy, or potential, electrical, or nuclear energy. In the end, all energy sources are natural. Sun, wind, rain, are gifts of nature, as are hay, horses, wood, coal, oil and gas - though their exploitation takes lesser or greater degrees of ingenuity and application. Until the modern era the principle sources of kinetic energy were manpower and horsepower, supplemented by some water- and wind-mills. Heating was mostly wood, with some coal; lighting meant the sun, or oil lamps.

The industrial revolution was marked by a shift from wood to coal, which is a better store of energy. In the 70 years from 1564 to 1634 coal shipments from Newcastle grew fourteen times to nearly half a million tons; total British output was 4 million tonnes in 1700, 10 million in 1800, 50 million in 1850, 230 million in 1900 - a growth in demand driven by the steam engine.[182] Newcomen's steam pump solved a flooding problem hitherto only tackled with horse-drawn pumps. Davy's safety lamp (1815) curbed explosions. Buddle's pump (1790) helped ventilation. Rails carried horse-drawn coal wagons.

Coal-heated steam replaced muscle- and horse-power. The one hundred million tons of coal Britons used in 1870 would generate the same amount of energy as would the calorific intake of a population of 850 million. The country's steam engines generated four million horsepower, or forty million manpower. That addition to the population would have eaten three times the country's wheat output.[183]

In the nineteenth century, sperm whale oil was the principle source of lighting and lubrication and in 1856 America produced 5 million tons of it. The invention of the kerosene lamp, burning refined 'coal oil', in 1857 signalled the high tide of the whale industry. In 1859

---

[182] Philip Sauvain, *British Economic and Social History*, p. 56
[183] David Landes, *The Unbound Prometheus*, Cambridge University Press, 1969, p. 97-8

Edwin Drake first drilled oil at Titusville, Pennsylvania, and the following year there were 30 kerosene plants in the US. In 1870 John D. Rockefeller floated Standard Oil on the stock exchange. The exploitation of oil in Iran, Saudi Arabia, Rumania, Azerbaijan, the North Sea, Venezuela and Nigeria fed the growing appetite for oil into the twenty-first century. Oil fields are created by the decay of anerobic decay of organic matter under the earth's surface, which also generates natural gas fields.

In 1919 US horse and mule use peaked at 20 million animals, at which time one fifth of all farmland was set aside to feed them. Then internal combustion engines displaced them as motive power for reapers, ploughs and combines.

In 1882 Thomas Edison, having perfected the electric light bulb, built the first power station in Pearl Street, providing direct current for lighting 59 homes in Manhattan. Earlier in the same year he had opened a steam-powered electricity generation station for street lighting at Holborn Viaduct. In 1886 George Westinghouse built the first Alternating Current generator, in Great Barrington, Massachusetts. Most power stations burned coal or oil and later natural gas. Hydro-electric power was generated at the Hoover Dam from 1936, and was coal-poor Italy's main source of electricity up till the Second World War.[184]

Marie Curie isolated radium in Paris, 1902, and Ernest Rutherford used a stream of radioactive particles to split the atom in 1919. Nuclear fission was developed as a weapon in the US Army's Manhattan Project, 1941-6. An experimental nuclear power generator was built in Idaho in 1951, and in 1955 in Obninsk in the Soviet Union nuclear power was first used to generate electricity for domestic use. The Sellafield nuclear power station was opened in 1956. As much as three quarters of French electricity was nuclear by the 1980s.[185]

---

[184] Vera Zamagni, *The Economic History of Italy 1860-1990,* Oxford, Clarendon Press, 1993, p. 93
[185] John Ardagh, *France in the New Century,* London, Penguin, 2000, p. 113

Transport

As commerce developed on the margins of nations, greater distances were covered in sea transport than on land in the renaissance world. With government support the merchant navy tripled its tonnage between 1629 and 1686 to 340,000 growing at 2.5 per cent a year from 1660 to 1690.[186] These sail-powered wooden-hulled ships were the first factories, turning goods in the wrong place into useful items. Early cargoes were high value items like spices, sugar, tea and sultanas, because profit on sale was the basis of the trade and journeys measured in months were a great investment.

On the 16 February 1870 the Cutty Sark left London with a cargo of wines, spirits and beer, returning from Shanghai with 1450 tons of tea on 13 October. But by then the opening of Suez Canal in 1869 gave the advantage to steam ships in the tea trade. In March 1802 the first steam tug, the Charlotte Dundas, built by William Symington pulled barges along the Forth and Clyde Canal, and in 1807 Robert Fulton began a steam passenger service from New York to Albany. Paddle steamers guzzled coal and had to fill their holds and decks with it. Still the Sirius was the first paddle steamer to cross the Atlantic in 1837 and as late as 1862 the Scotia won the blue riband for crossing from Queenstown, Ireland to New York in the record time of eight days. John Ericsson fitted the first screw propeller to an Atlantic-crossing ship in 1839. Isambard Kingdom Brunel built the propeller-driven, iron-hulled ship, the Great Britain in 1843 adding capacity to fuel efficiency. In 1852 the Great Britain matched the Yankee wooden clippers' 80 days for the journey from Liverpool to Melbourne, but carrying 630 passengers and a crew of 137.[187] Compound engines and Parsons steam turbine cut journey time further.

In 1878 the Paraguay carried 80 tons of mutton frozen by a machine built by Ferdinand Carré from Argentina to Marseilles, a journey of 50 days. Two years later the Strathleven carried beef chilled with a machine made by Bell and Coleman from Melbourne to London

---

[186] Peter Linebaugh and Marcus Rediker, *The Many-Headed Hydra,* Boston, Beacon Press, 2000 p. 146
[187] Geoffrey Blainey, *The Tyranny of Distance,* p. 212-3

in 57 days, advertising her wares with an on-board banquet.[188] In 1900 Britain imported 360,000 metric tonnes of meat, from Argentina (220,000) New Zealand (95,000) and Australia (45,000). Diesel engines, first used by the MS Selandia in 1912 - and Amundsen's arctic ship later that year - were common after the First World War. In 1914 the world's shipping fleet could carry 45 million tonnes; that grew to 85 million in 1950, 227 million in 1970, 553 million in 2000. Today the largest container ships carry 90,000 tonnes, 8000 containers-full, with a crew of just nineteen.[189]

Goods were transported around Britain by boat, and where possible inland on rivers, though these were often poor. In 1773 the Duke of Bridgwater opened the canal linking Manchester to the Mersey, a year after its chief engineer James Brindley died. One horse could draw eight tons on a level railway, but 65 tons on a barge, cutting transport costs. Between 1760 and 1840 Britain enjoyed a canal boom that left 6400km of navigable inland waterways. In the United States the Erie Canal opened in 1825 connected the Hudson River, and therefore New York City to Lake Erie. The Great Lakes were united by canals like the Sault Ste. Marie creating by 1886 a great system tying Duluth, Chicago, Detroit, Cleveland and Buffalo to trade with the Eastern Atlantic seaboard.[190]

British road 'navigators' like 'blind Jack' Metcalf (1717-1810) and Thomas Telford (1757-1834) developed inland travel in the early nineteenth century. Scotsman John Macadam developed the system of compounded aggregate road surfacing (Macadam, 1820) later bound with tar (tarmac, invented by Edgar Purnell Hooley in 1902).

Coalmines had already pioneered the use of wooden rails, and in 1767 Darby's Coalbrookdale Works made iron ones. It was there that Richard Trevithick's first locomotive engine worked from 1803. In 1825 George Stephenson's *Locomotion* became the first steam passenger train, on the newly built Stockton to Darlington line; four years later George and his son Robert Stephenson won the competition

---

[188] Blainey, *The Tyranny of Distance*, p. 278
[189] David Edgerton, *The Shock of the Old*, p. 74
[190] Frederick Jackson Turner, *The Frontier in American History,* Tucson, University of Arizona Press, 1994, pp. 136, 150

to work the Liverpool to Manchester line with the Rocket. Within a month the railway was carrying 1200 people a day, and quickly the company started carrying merchandise as well. Alongside the Stephensons' lines, Isambard Kingdom Brunel built the Great Western Railway, laying over 1500 km of track. Engineers today agree that Brunel's wide gauge track is safer and more efficient, but Stephenson's narrow gauge, once laid on the 1838 London to Birmingham line won the day.[191] Parliament ruled the narrow gauge standard, so integrating the national railways in 1846.

US railroads followed Indian trading trails. In the 1850s the railroads first linked the Mississippi to the North Atlantic seaboard and New Orleans gave way to New York as the outlet for the Mid-west farm goods.[192] In May 1869 two armies of mixed Irish and Chinese 'coolie' labourers met at Ogden, Utah to drive the last spike of the Union Pacific Railroad, connecting the two seaboards.[193] In 1920 the historian of the American Frontier Frederick Jackson Turner marvelled that passengers doubled, and freight trebled between 1890 and 1908, then doubled again between 1908 and 1919.[194] Australia, failing to heed the advice of the British government, failed to standardise railway gauges until the 1880s, when building boomed: in 1875 there were just 1600 miles of rail, but by 1875 that jumped to 10,000, and in 1921 peaked at 26,000.[195] Economists estimated that carrying a ton of goods 100 miles in New South Wales by horse cost £5 in 1898, but by rail just 18s.5d, or 92 pence. The first railways were built in India in 1853 and by 1880 they extended 9000 miles connecting the interior to the ports at Bombay, Calcutta and Madras.

The Scotsman Robert Davidson built the first (battery-powered) electric locomotive in 1837, and in 1879 an electric passenger service ran in Berlin. It was only with mainline electrification that trains could be run successfully following the example of the Baltimore Belt Line in 1895.

---

[191] Philip Sauvain, *British Economic and Social History*, p. 128-9
[192] Frederick Jackson Turner, *The Frontier in American History*, p. 137
[193] Lewis Corey, *House of Morgan,* New York, Grosset and Dunlap, 1930, p. 101
[194] Turner, *The Frontier in American History*, p. 314
[195] Geoffrey Blainey, *The Tyranny of Distance*, p. 263

In 1862 the Metropolitan Railway became the first underground line, built on the cut and cover method. It spread to Bayswater in 1868 and reached Harrow by 1880. In 1870 the first underground railway tunnel running under the Thames from Tower Hill to Vine Street was built. Workmen were encouraged to use trams with cut-price tickets, and the first cable tram connected Highgate Hill and Archway in 1891.

Around 1885, the first 'safety bicycles', that is chain-driven, unlike the high 'Penny-farthings' whose pedals were fixed on the front wheel, were developed. In 1888 Ulsterman John Dunlop, out of concern for his son, came up with the pneumatic tire for his bicycle, while Lechner perfected the ball-bearing in 1898. Michaux the pedal in 1861 and Trefz chain transmission in 1869.[196] The combination made cycling safe and fun leading to a bicycle-craze that saw production reach 1.2 million a year by the mid-1890s.[197] Peaking in the developed countries, world-wide bicycle production is around 100 million a year.[198]

In 1886 Daimler and Benz mounted an internal combustion engine on a carriage to make the first motor-car. Henry Ford made the Model-T from 1908 to 1927 turning out fifteen million cars and trucks.[199] Mass car ownership in Europe had to wait till after the Second World War, so in Italy car ownership increased from 340,000 to 4.7 million cars between 1950 and 1964.[200] By 2002 there were ten million private cars in China.[201] Annual car production worldwide stands at 40 million.[202]

In 1903, Orville Wright's internal combustion engine powered plane flew for just a few feet, opening a new era of air travel. After the Second World War, the use of gas turbine engines brought faster and safer jet flight. The Atlantic crossing was down to eight hours, from eight days by steam ship; the flight to Australia reduced from eighty days by clipper to one.

---

[196] Umberto Eco, *From the Plough to Polaris,* New York, Macmillan, 1963, p.284
[197] Hounshell, *From the American System to Mass Production,* p.200-01
[198] Edgerton, *The Shock of the Old,* p. 45
[199] Hounshell, *From the American System to Mass Production,* p. 219
[200] Edgerton, *The Shock of the Old,* p. 69
[201] *State of the World,* London, W. W. Norton, 2004, p. 3
[202] Edgerton, *The Shock of the Old,* p. 45

Materials

Developments in machinery and engines were dependent on those in metals. Though iron and steel manufacture were both pre-modern, cast iron was brittle and steel difficult to make. Abraham Darby's Coalbrookdale works perfected pig-iron casting with coke which was less brittle (1709) and in 1784 Henry Cort stirred, or 'puddled' molten iron, then beat it to make it more supple. Cort's puddled pig iron was much more efficient and output increased from 70,000 tonnes in 1786 to 2.25 million tonnes in 1850. In 1740 Benjamin Huntsman burned off the carbon, silicon and manganese in iron in a clay crucible to make steel, but it was not until Henry Bessemer blew air through molten iron to burn off the impurities in his Converter in 1855 that durable steel could be mass-produced.

In 1869 John Hyatt created the first synthetic plastic, *celluloid*, from wood pulp. The chemical generation of plastics, mostly from chains of organic molecules called polymers opened a new era of malleable materials. After celluloid, the Belgian American Leo Baekeland made *bakelite* in 1908 as a replacement for Shellac, a resin taken from beetles. Bakelite, made by combining phenol and formaldehyde and splitting off the water molecules, proved to be a much more durable material, which could be moulded before it hardened on cooling and gave good insulation for radios, telephones and electric plugs. The Dupont Company unveiled nylon at the 1939 World Fair, around the same time that Bayer were perfecting polyurethane and another Du Pont chemist Roy Plunkett came up with Teflon.

A.G. Wayss in Germany and Thadeus Hyatt in the United States both started to make building systems using concrete reinforced with metal bars in the 1870s, on a technique first tried out by the Frenchman Joseph Louis Lambert. This 'ferro-concrete' carried much greater weight than ordinary concrete, so that buildings could go higher, bridges wider and motorway flyovers longer.

Agriculture

At the dawn of the factory age, agriculture was already undergoing a revolution mostly due to the forced consolidation of private property in the Acts of Enclosure. These were viciously unjust for the small farmers who lost out. The concentration of land allowed the introduction of improvements in tool-use (like the 1760 Rotherham Plough, or Jethro Tull's 1701 seed drill or Andrew Meikle's threshing machine of 1786), selective breeding, crop-rotation (to mitigate soil-exhaustion, pioneered by Viscount 'Turnip' Townshend from 1730) and the use of natural fertilisers.

The separation of town and country transformed agriculture. Railways carried farm produce to feed the towns, demand that increased incomes to buy new farm implements like sickles, iron ploughs and reaping machines. In 1866 railways carried 43,400 litres of milk to London.[203] Steam-powered traction engines, and then later motorisation transformed farming. Family-run American farms took up cars (eighty percent had them by 1930) even faster than tractors (30 per cent) or trucks. In Britain, increased productivity meant fewer agricultural labourers fed more people: in 1851 there were 2 million out of a population of 20 million; by 1871 agricultural labourers were down to 1.8 million though the population had risen to 26 million.[204] An American farmer in 1900 fed seven people; today his great grandson feeds 667 people.[205] In the 1960s, dependent on food aid, India commissioned Cambridge scientist M. S Swaminathan to introduce the high yield crops and fertilisers that created the country's 'green revolution'. World grain output rose from 400 million tons in 1900 to 1.9 billion tons in 1998.[206] As a share of household income, spending

---

[203] Philip Sauvain, *British Economic and Social History*, p. 36
[204] Sauvain, *British Economic and Social History*, p. 36
[205] James Heartfield, 'Two Cheers for Agribusiness', *Review of Radical Political Economy*, 32, 2, 2000, p.319
[206] Lester Brown, *The State of the World*, London, Earthscan, 1999, p. 115; US Bureau of Labor Statistics, http://www.bls.gov/oes/current/oes_nat.htm#b45-0000

on food and clothes fell from one third to just over a tenth in Europe and America between 1950 and 2000, because of cheaper agriculture.

Food processing

For millennia food has been preserved by pickling, salting, sugaring and fermenting. In the modern era the demands of food transportation encouraged new innovations. Napoleon's army first experimented with cooked and then vacuum-packed, tinned goods. In 1875 Henry Heinz exploited the developments of the pressure cooker (the previous year) and the use of calcium chloride to accelerate sterilization time and improvements in canning to set out to become the largest food processor in the US by 1900, and a world company with a $9 billion turnover today.[207] Later mechanized cooling and freezing devices transformed the preservation of meats and vegetables. Chemical additives like Sodium Benzoate are used today.

Retail and distribution

Working-class shoppers formed buyers' cooperative in Scotland and England to keep prices down as far back as the 1760s, and in 1844 the Co-operative Society opened its first shop in Rochdale.[208] Those 'Rochdale Pioneers' set the model for the first supermarket, the Co-operative Retail Society which still turns over £7 billion in Britain each year.[209] Innovators like Nottingham's Jesse Boot (who founded Boots in 1883), Glasgow's Thomas Lipton (est. 1871) W.H. Smith and Son (that secured the railway bookstore franchise in 1841), Leeds trader Michael Marks who teamed with Manchester cashier Thomas Spencer in 1904 - all rode to success on the growth in working class consumption. Today the supermarket Tesco's, built on the late Jack

---

[207] Nancy Koehn, *Brand New,* Boston, Harvard Business School, 2001, p. 90
[208] W. Hamish Fraser, *The Coming of the Mass Market 1850-1914,* London, Macmillan, 1981, p. 121
[209] Andrew Simm, *Tescopoly,* London, Constable, 2007, p. 71

Cohen's motto 'Stack it high, sell it cheap', is Britain's most successful retailer with 12.5 per cent of the retail trade, 31 per cent of the grocery market and 250,000 employees in the UK.

In the US, F.W. Woolworth opened the first 'five and ten cent' store in Lancaster, Pennsylvania in 1879. Marshall Field opened what was then the world's largest department store in Chicago in 1902.[210] In 1893 Richard Sears and Alvah Roebuck started the pre-eminent catalogue company Sears and Roebuck following Montgomery Ward's business model. The Singer Sewing Machine Company understood the relative importance of distribution to production, employing twice as many sales staff (61,444 world wide in 1905) as manufacturers.[211] In the 1950s Earl Tupper and Brownie Wise marketed plastic foods boxes with 'tupperware parties' - a model successfully followed by Avon Cosmetics and Ann Summers' sex toys.

Daventry International Rail Freight Terminal Logistics Park (see above) is three and a half hours from eighty-five per cent of the UK. Through DIRFT, Tesco's 'distribute frozen foods to 70 per cent of the UK, and distribute 6500 different clothing product lines to more than 770 outlets', according to their IT and logistics director, Philip Clarke. In DIRFT, and nearby, Tesco has one million square feet of warehousing, including freezer space equivalent to 23 million domestic freezers. The Royal Mail built a 262 500 ft^2 cross dock processing centre there to rationalise their national transport network. Asda Wal Mart runs six trains to Grangemouth in Scotland – just some of the 120 trains out of Dirft each week. But despite the historical importance of trains and canals in transporting consumer goods, today 82 per cent of all freight goes on roads, while just eight per cent goes by rail. 'Lorries deliver 4.5 million tonnes of freight each day, approximately 80 kgs per person' which is 'more that the average body weight' according to Alan McKinnon of Heriot-Watt University's Logistics Research Centre. According to McKinnon, without lorries on the roads, supermarkets,

---

[210] Nancy Koehn, *Brand New*, p. 91
[211] David Edgerton, *The Shock of the Old*, p. 58

industry, petrol stations, hospitals and schools would all be out of action within one week.[212]

Construction

In 1847 the Metropolitan Commissioner of Sewers directed that all waste be carried in closed sewers down to the Thames, but though well intentioned this was a disaster, overloading the river with sewage. In 1858 London was beset by a 'Great Stink'. At that time there were three million Londoners depending on the Thames to carry their effluent away. 61,000 died from cholera in 1848-9, then 26,000 died in 1853-4 (10,000 in the capital) and then in 1866 17,000 died (6000 in the capital). But already in 1855 Joseph Bazalgette had begun the scheme to direct the waste away from the Thames building 165 miles of main sewer (in Portland cement) with some 1100 miles of local sewers. What Bazalgette did in London, Birmingham's Lord Mayor Joseph Chamberlain did there. By 1870 146 out of 180 towns used sewers instead of cesspools, but then only 46 treated the sewage before putting in back into the rivers – as all do today. By 1901 90 per cent of provincial towns provided their own waters. Glasgow, Liverpool, Birmingham and Manchester all supplied water from distant sources free from contamination.

In 1883, Emily Warren Roebling oversaw the completion the Brooklyn Bridge, then the world's longest suspension bridge at 6000 feet (1595 feet at its longest span) that had been designed by her father-in-law 13 years earlier. John Roebling had been a student of the German philosopher Hegel and applied rational principles to construction, though injury cost him his life, and Emily's husband Washington was crippled with Caisson's disease digging under pressure to find bedrock for the Washington Tower.

Ferdinand de Lesseps oversaw 36,000 Egyptian corvée labourers digging the Suez Canal 1859-69,[213] which carried more than

---

[212] Alan Mackinnon, 'Life without lorries, The impact of a temporary disruption to road freight transport in the UK', *Commercial Motor,* November 2004, p 21

[213] Magali Morsy, *North Africa, 1800-1900,* New York, Longman, 1984, p. 174

120 million tonnes of merchandise in 1955. De Lesseps began work on the Panama Canal in 1882, but the 82 km waterway was only completed in 1914 under US govt. supervision. The canal reduces the route from San Francisco to New York by 12,500km.

The Hoover Dam, on the Colorado River, completed under Elwood Mead's supervision in 1935 is 221m high and 379m wide. Built in 1970 the Aswan High Dam on the Nile can generate 2.1 gigaWatts of electricity.[214]

Public health

Real advances in medicine are few and far between Hippocrates' day and the eighteenth century, regimes of care accounting for most of its successes. In 1796 Edward Jenner, on hearing that cows-maids were resistant to Smallpox, undertook the first vaccination, using Cowpox as a vaccine against the deadly disease. In 1865 Louis Pasteur investigating a disease in silk worms developed the germ theory. Before him Dr John Snow established that Cholera was water borne studying the infection of 17 families in Albion Terrace, Wandsworth Road, whose waste pipes were backed up, infecting their water supply.[215] On the basis of Pasteur's insight, Lister, a surgeon in Scotland developed the first anti-sceptic regime cutting the high mortality in hospitals.[216] Pasteur developed vaccines for anthrax and viral rabies. Jonas Salk developed the first polio vaccine in 1955 and in 1963 a vaccination for measles was found. In 1922 Alexander Fleming identified that the mould *Penicillium notarium* inhibited some bacteria, creating the first of many antibiotics. In the 1980s Australian Doctors Marshall and Warren discovered the bacteria *Helicobacter pylori* was responsible for many stomach ulcers, opening the way to antibiotic treatment of this previously chronic condition.

---

[214] http://www.mbarron.net/Nile/envir_nf.html
[215] John Snow, *On the Mode of Communication of Cholera,* London, 1849
[216] J. D. Bernal, *Science and History,* London, Watts and Co., p. 473

Telecommunications

Static electricity had been used to communicate messages as early as 1737, but it was Danish physicist Hans Oersted's discovery of the effect of electric current on a compass that helped Samuel Morse create the telegraph in 1844. Its spread was spurred by railways. In 1866 William Thompson, Lord Kelvin oversaw the laying of the Atlantic cable that connected Wall Street with the City of London,[217] and in 1871 the Society of Telegraph Engineers was incorporated. In 1876 Alexander Bell made the first telephone at Boston University (though some claim Italian Antonio Meucci was first), founding the Bell Telephone Company the next year. In 1952 Narinder Singh Kapany developed the first optical fibres which carry much more information than copper wire. In 1897 Gugliemo Marconi demonstrated radio telegraphy over 19 km and by 1901 radio transmissions were being received across the Atlantic.

In 1967 the US Advance Research Project Association under J. Licklider started work on the ARPANET connecting up computers for synchronous discussion. With some finessing, like Donald Watts' packet-switching technology and Cerf and Kahn's Transmission Control Protocol (1974), ARPANET laid the basis for the modern internet, which can best be dated from the National Science Foundation's university-wide NSFnet in 1983. In Cern in 1991, Tim Berners Lee developed the html and http interface that built the World Wide Web on top of the internet.

Computerisation

'I wish to God these calculations had been executed by steam', said Charles Babbage checking astronomical charts in 1821.[218] In 1642 Blaise Pascal invented an arithmetic calculating machine and Liebniz 1694 calculator could multiply, divide and extract square roots.

---

[217] Bernal, *Science and History*, p. 390
[218] Doron Swade, *The Difference Engine*, New York, Viking, 2000, p. 9

Some key dates in computerisation

Pre-1950: Konrad Zuse, a German engineer, completes the first general purpose progammable calculator in 1941. He pioneers the use of binary math and Boolean logic in electronic calculation.
1945: 'As We May Think' published by Vannevar Bush in The *Atlantic Monthly*
1950: Alan Turing proposes the 'Turing test' criterion for an intelligent machine
1951: UNIVAC, the Universal Automatic Computer, is developed. It can store 12,000 digits in random access mercury-delay lines.
Presper Eckert and John Mauchly finish UNIVAC I, the first mass-produced electronic computer
1953: IBM 650 is the first mass-produced computer
LEO [the Lyons Electronic Office] (the first commercial version of EDSAC) is launched [by the Lyons company]
1955: IBM engineers jointly develop magnetic core storage units, a dramatic improvement over cathode-ray tube memory technology.
1956: IBM introduces the Random Access Method of Accounting and Control (RAMAC) hard drive, with a capacity of 5MB and weighing over a ton
1957: Unix development begins at Bell Labs.
1958: Modem data phone developed at Bell Labs
1960: DEC introduces PDP-1, first commercial computer with keyboard and monitor
1960 'Man-Computer Symbiosis' by JCR Licklider published
1962: JCR Licklider describes his 'Galactic Network' concept, the first recorded description of the social interactions that could be enabled through networking.
1962: Douglas Englebart's paper 'Augmenting Human Intellect: A Conceptual Framework' published
1962: First video game
1962: Ivan Sutherland demonstrates a program called Sketchpad on a TX-2 mainframe at MIT's Lincoln Labs in 1962. It allows him to make engineering drawings with a light pen.
1963: Claude E Shannon and Warren Weaver publish 'The Mathematical Theory of Communication' (University of Illinois Press, 1963) which contends that all communication is essentially digital.
1964: Paul Baran, working at the Rand Corporation, publishes his ideas about a distributed network.
1964: The [third generation] IBM 360 is introduced in April of 1964 and quickly becomes the standard institutional mainframe computer. By the mid-80s the 360 and its descendents will have generated more than $100 billion in revenue for IBM.
1964: Mouse demonstrated: by Douglas Engelbart
1965: Moore's Law: An IC that cost $1000 in 1959 now costs less than $10. Gordon Moore predicts that the number of components in an IC will double every year.

Heartfield *Green Capitalism*

> 1965: Ted Nelson coins the phrases 'hypertext', referring to text that diverges and allows choice to the reader, that's best read at an interactive screen.
> 1966: Donald Davies gives public lecture on packets, told about Baran's work
> 1968: Doug Engelbart, working at the Stanford Research Institute, demonstrates a word processor, an early hypertext system and a collaborative application: three now common computer applications.
> 1970: ARPANET goes online: connecting Stanford and UCLA.
> 1972: Intel launches the 8008, an 8-bit microprocessor, and 8080
> 1975: Popular Electronics features the MITS Altair 8800 on its cover, January 1975. It is hailed as the first 'personal' computer. Thousands of orders for the 8800 rescue MITS from bankruptcy.
> 1976: Jobs and Wozniak build Apple I
> 1979: Software Arts develops the first spreadsheet program, Visicalc, by the spring of 1979. It is released in October and is an immediate success. Copies shipped per month rise from 500 to 12,000 between 1979 and 1981.
> 1980: IBM adopts MS DOS as PC OS
> 1980: First commercial database program: dBase II by Ratcliff
> 1984: The Apple Macintosh debuts. It features a simple, graphical interface, uses the 8-MHz, 32-bit Motorola 68000 CPU, and has a built-in 9-inch B/W screen.
> 1985: Intel 386 chipset launched with 32-bit processing
> 1989: Intel launches 486 chipset
> 1989: Microsoft launches Windows 3.0
> 1991: Linus Torvalds builds first version of Linux
> January 1993: Marc Andreessen and Eric Bina release a point-and-click graphical browser for the Web, designed to run on Unix machines, called Mosaic.
> 1994, December: Netscape Communications Netscape Navigator 1.0 browser launched by Mosaic Communications, founded by Jim Clark and Marc Andreesen
>
> Prepared by Nico MacDonald

Babbage's own Difference Engine (a portion of which was assembled by Joseph Clement in 1832) and Analytical Engine were never completed.

Vannevar Bush built the first analog computer (where mechanical movement corresponded to calculations), the Differential Analyser in 1930. Herman Hollerith at the US Census office had used punch cards to tabulate the 1890 census, and in 1938 Claude Shannon showed how logical operations could correspond to on/off circuit switches. In 1937 Howard Aiken made the Automatic Sequence-Controlled Calculator for IBM, which used punched paper tape and was effectively the first digital computer. Eckert and Mauchly built the first completely electronic computer (ENIAC - Electronic Numeric Integrator and Computer) in 1943 and John von Neumann built the first programmable computer (EDVAC Electronic Discrete Variable Automatic Computer) in 1947. In 1948 Bell Telephone Laboratories replaced the valve with the transistor starting the revolution in scale that would make computers ubiquitous, and in 1947 M.I.T. developed the first magnetic core memory.[219]

Acculturation

The revolution in productive technique over the last two and a half centuries did not only change the tools we use, it changed the world we live in and it changed us. Modern men and women are the same species as homo sapiens before them, but they are thoroughly different people.

To take the simplest first, the world population grew from 791 million in 1750 to 5.9 billion in 1999. A small part of that addition would have been possible on the existing level of technology, but most of those 5.1 billion people owe their existence to improvements in agriculture, industry, transport, water and sewage management and medicine. In the US, life expectancy increased from 47 to 77 between 1900 and 2000; in China the increase was even greater, from 35 in 1950 to 71 in 2000; in India it was 32 in 1950, 64 in 2000. Even in Africa, that most troubled of continents in recent times, life expectancy rose above 50. These improvements in life expectancy can only mean that the world economy is succeeding at the most basic level to generate subsistence for six billion human beings.

On 1 July 1916 the Accrington Pals were marched into machine gun fire, killing 235 and wounding 530. For most of them, it was the first time they had left their northern town. Up until the 1840s, Inuit in Greenland and Canada would spend their entire lives without meeting anyone but another Inuit. Today's world is overwhelmingly cosmopolitan by contrast. Tourist travel grows year on year, internet

---

[219] Jasia Reichardt, *Robots,* London, Thames and Hudson, 1978, p. 154-7

connections are growing more quickly in China than the United States, and South Korea has the greatest broadband penetration on the planet.

Our world has been transformed. In the nineteenth century the oceans were transformed from barriers into thoroughfares; in the twentieth the sky was so changed. Distances have been collapsed. Throughout the twentieth century, people have left the land, liberated from drudgery, to be thrust into a turbulent cosmopolitan lifestyle. Goods that just a few years ago were unheard of are today looked on as necessities, such as mobile phones or even iPods.

In intellectual life mass literacy has transformed society. In 1841 33 per cent of men and 44 per cent of women in Britain signed their marriage certificates with a mark. Today 130 out of 179 countries have a literacy rate higher than 70 per cent. China's is 93 per cent, India's 61 per cent, North America, Russia, West and Eastern Europe are all above 90 per cent.

The basic ideas of Martin Luther, John Locke, Adam Smith, Jean-Jacques Rousseau, John Stuart Mill, Karl Marx, Charles Darwin, the romantic poets, Sigmund Freud, V. I. Lenin, Martin Luther King, Sociology, Surrealism, the stream-of-consciousness, neo-classical economics, method acting, women's liberation, Frantz Fanon, ecology and Al Qaeda are all in principle accessible and intelligible to a substantial share of the world's population in a way they never could have been without mass literacy.

Bibliography

Organisations consulted:

Bonobo Initiative
British Petroleum
Department for Environment Food and Rural Affairs (was Department of the Environment, Transport and the Regions)
Economic Research Service/USDA,
Energy Information Administration
House of Commons Environmental Audit Committee
http://www.houseprices.uk.net,
National Statistics
Reuters
Sustainable Energy and Economy Network
Tennessee Centre for Policy Research
World Wildlife Fund

Publications consulted

BBC Online
Boston Phoenix
Fast Company Magazine
Financial Times
Guardian
Independent
International Herald Tribune
International Socialist Journal
MoneyWeek,
New Left Review
New York Times
Observer
PR Watch Newsletter,
Private Eye,
Spiked-online.com
Sunday Times

Sydney Morning Herald
The Times
Town and Country Planning
USA Today
Washington Post

Books and Articles

Ardagh, John, *France in the New Century,* London, Penguin, 2000
Arnold Ron and Alan Gottlieb, *Trashing the Economy,* Washington D.C., Merril Press, 1994
Bernal, J. D., *Science and History,* London, Watts and Co.
Blainey, Geoffrey, *The Tyranny of Distance,* Sydney, Macmillan, 2001
Brandt, Willy, *North-South: A Programme for Survival,* Independent Commission on International Development Issues London, Pan, 1980, (the Brandt Report)
Brown, Lester, *Building a Sustainable Community,* New York, Worldwatch Institute, 1981
Brown, Lester, *The State of the World,* London, Earthscan, 1999
Bruegmann, Robert, *Sprawl: a compact history,* Chicago, University Press, 2005
Cannan, Edwin, 'The Origin Of The Law Of Diminishing Returns', 1813-15, *Economic Journal,* vol. 2, 1892
Chandler David and Gideon Baker, *Constructing Global Civil Society,* London, Palgrave, 2005
Clinton, Bill, *My Life,* New York, Random House, 2005
Corey, Lewis, *House of Morgan,* New York, Grosset and Dunlap, 1930
Cox W. Michael and Richard Alm, *Myths of Rich and Poor: why we're better off than we think,* New York, Basic Books 1999
Cox, Wendell, *War on the Dream,* Lincoln, iUniverse, 2006
DeLong Brad, 'Estimating World GDP', http://econ161.berkeley.edu/TCEH/1998_Draft/World_GDP/Estimating_World_GDP.html
Demographia, Second Annual Demographia Survey, Belleville, 2006

Department of Trade and Industry, *UK Productivity and competitiveness indicators,* DTI Paper no 9, 2003
Driessen, Paul, *Eco-Imperialism,* Washington, Merril Press, 2004
Eco, Umberto, *From the Plough to Polaris,* New York, Macmillan, 1963
Edgerton, David, *The Shock of the Old,* London, Profile, 2006
Esty, D. C., *Green to Gold,* New Haven, Yale University Press, 2006
France, Peter, *The Charter of the Land,* Melbourne, Oxford University Press, 1969
Fraser, W. Hamish, *The Coming of the Mass Market 1850-1914,* London, Macmillan, 1981
Gilder, George, *Microcosm: the quantum revolution in economics and technology,* New York, Simon and Schuster, 1990
Gingrich, Newt, *A Contract with the Earth,* Baltimore, John Hopkins University Press, 2007
Gourevitch, Alex, 'Better living through chemistry', *Atlantic Monthly,* March 2003
Gray, John, *Straw Dogs: thoughts on humans and other animals,* London, Granta, 2003
Gruber, Jacob, 'Ethnographic Salvage and the Shaping of Anthropology', *American Anthropologist,* Vol 72, no. 6, 1970
Halliday, Jon, *A Political History of Japanese Capitalism,* New York, Monthly Review Press, 1975
Hamilton-Paterson, James, *America's Boy,* London, Granta, 1999
Hearn, Julie, 'African NGOs: the new compradors?' *Development and Change,* Volume 38 Issue 6 Page 1095-1110, November 2007
Heartfield, James, 'Two Cheers for Agri-Business', *Review of Radical Political Economics,* 32, 2, 2000
Heartfield, James, *Let's Build! Why we need five million new homes in the next 10 years,* London, Audacity, 2006
Henwood, Doug, *After the New Economy,* New York, New Press, 2005
Herbst, Moira *Labor Research* 5 July 2005
Hounshell, David, *From the American System to Mass Production,* Baltimore, John Hopkins UP, 1984,
Inglehart Ronald and Paul Abramson, *Value Change in Global Perspective,* Michigan, University Press, 1995

International Rivers Network, 'The case for rivers', http://www.irn.org/dayofaction/index.php?id=background5.html, viewed on 14 December 2007
Irvine, Sandy, 'The Prophet Misarmed: Trotsky, Ecology and Sustainability', *What Next?* 31, 2007
Isaacs, Harold, *The Tragedy of the Chinese Revolution,* Stanford UP, 1961
Jacobs, Michael, *The Politics of the Real World,* London, Earthscan, 1996
Jowell, R. et al. (eds), *British and European Social Attitudes: How Britain Differs: The 15th Report,* Aldershot, Ashgate Publishing, 1998
Kasapoglu, M. Aytulk and Mehmet Ecevit, 'Attitudes and behaviour towards the Environment', *Environment and Behavior,* Vol. 34, No. 3, 363-377 (2002)
Kennedy, Paul, *The Rise and Fall of the Great Powers,* London, Fontana, 1990
Koehn, Nancy, *Brand New,* Boston, Harvard Business School, 2001
Labour Party, *Let Us Work Together – Labour's Way Out of the Crisis,* London, 1974
Labour Party, *The New Hope for Britain,* London, 1983
Landes, David, *The Unbound Prometheus,* Cambridge University Press, 1969
Leadbeater, Charles, *Living on Thin Air*, London, Penguin, 2000
Linebaugh Peter and Marcus Rediker, *The Many-Headed Hydra,* Boston, Beacon Press, 2000
Lloyd, Daniel, 'Paper on Consumer Regulation for CBI', c. 2006
Lovins, Amory, L. Hunter Lovins and Ernst von Wiezsacker, *Factor Four: Doubling wealth, halving resource use,* London, Earthscan
Mackinnon, Alan, 'Life without lorries, The impact of a temporary disruption to road freight transport in the UK', *Commercial Motor,* November 2004
Macnaghten, Phil and John Urry, *Contested Natures,* London, Sage, 1998
Maren, Michael, *The Road to Hell,* New York, The Free Press, 1997
Mariategui, Jose Carlos, *The Heroic and Creative Meaning of Socialism,* Humanities Press, NJ, 1996

Marx, Karl, *Capital,* Vol. I, Moscow, Progress, 1974
Marx, Karl, *Capital,* Vol. III, London, Lawrence and Wishart, 1959
Marx, Karl, *Grundrisse,* Harmondsworth, Penguin, 1973
Mehring, Franz, *Absolutism and Revolution in Germany,* London, 1975, New Park,
Mermelstein, David (ed), *Economics,* Random House, New York, 1973
Meszaros, Istvan, *The Necessity of Social Control,* London, Merlin, 1971
Mishan, E. J., *The Costs of Economic Growth,* Harmondsworth, Penguin, 1979
Monbiot, George, *Heat,* London, Penguin, 2006
Morsy, Magali, *North Africa, 1800-1900,* New York, Longman, 1984
Mumford, Stephen, *The Life and Death of NSSM 200,* N Carolina, Centre for Research on Population and Security, 1996
Naomi Klein, *No Logo,* London, Flamingo, 2000
Nworah, Kenneth, 'The Aborigines Protection Society', *Canadian Journal of African Studies,* Vol. 5, No.1 86
Office of National Statistics, *Britain 2000,* London, HMSO
Perelman Michael, *Steal this Idea,* New York, Palgrave Macmillan, 2002
Perelman Michael, *The Invention of Capitalism,* Durham, Duke University Press, 2000
Reichardt, Jasia, *Robots,* London, Thames and Hudson, 1978
Sahlins, Marshall, *Stone Age Economics.* Hawthorne, NY, 1972
Sartre, Jean-Paul, *Critique of Dialectical Reason,* London, Verso, 1991
Sauvain, Philip, *British Economic and Social History,* Cheltenham, Stanley Thornes, 1987
Schmidt, Alfred, *The Concept of nature in Marx,* London, Verso,
Shell International Limited, *There is No Alternative,* London, 2002
Simm, Andrew, *Tescopoly,* London, Constable, 2007
Smith, Ian, *The Great Betrayal,* London, Blake Publishing, 1997
Smith, Margaret Laws, *Towards the Creation of a Sustainable Economy,* London, Conservation Society, 1975
Snow, John, *On the Mode of Communication of Cholera,* London, 1849
Smil, Vaclav, *Energy,* Oxford, One World, 2006

Stoll, David, *Rigoberta Menchu and the Story of all Poor Guatemalans,* Boulder, Westview Press, 1999

Swade, Doron, *The Difference Engine,* New York, Viking, 2000

Tang, Kenny and Ruth Yeoh, *Cut Carbon, grow profits,* London, Middlesex University Press, 2007

Tansley, Arthur, 'The use and abuse of vegetational concepts and terms', *Ecology,* Vol. 16, No. 3, July 1935

Trotsky, Leon, *If America Should Go Communist,* 1934, http://www.marxists.org/archive/trotsky/1934/08/ame.htm, viewed on 14 December 2007

Trotsky, Leon, *Permanent Revolution,* Introduction to the German edition, http://www.marxists.org/archive/trotsky/1931/tpr/prge.htm, viewed on 14 December 2007

Trotsky, Leon, *The History of the Russian Revolution,* London, Pluto, 1985

Trotsky, Leon, *The Revolution Betrayed,* New York, Pathfinder Press, 1972

Turner, Frederick Jackson, *The Frontier in American History,* Tucson, University of Arizona Press, 1994

Wambugu, Dr Florence, 'Biotechnology in Africa', 26 March 2003, http://www.bio.org/foodag/action/20030326.asp, viewed on 14 December 2007

Wolton, Suke, *Lord Hailey, the Colonial Office and the Politics of Race and Empire in the Second World War,* London, Macmillan, 2000

Worldwatch Institute, *State of the World,* London, W. W. Norton, 2004

Zamagni, Vera, *The Economic History of Italy 1860-1990,* Oxford, Clarendon Press, 1993

Zeller, Christian, 'From the Gene to the Globe', *Review of International Political Economy* 15:1 February 2008: 86–115

Index

Aboriginal Protection Society,	79-80
Africa,	75, 76, 77
African National Congress,	80
Agriculture,	42-4, 75-7
Air travel,	53-5
Amazon,	23, 41, 77, 82
'Appropriate technology',	71-3, 75
Australia,	45
Bagehot, Walter,	84
Bali climate talks,	68
Barclays,	26
Barratt Homes,	24, 47
BedZed housing complex,	64-5
Ben & Jerry's,	25
Blair, Tony,	26
Blue Circle,	31
Body Shop,	23, 51
Bonobo Initiative,	41
Borlaug, Norman,	75
Bovine Spongiform Encephalopathy (BSE),	52
British American Tobacco,	30
British Broadcasting Corporation (BBC),	23, 24, 54, 63
British Gas,	15
British Petroleum,	30, 31, 35
British Rail,	15
Brown, Gordon,	82
Brown, Lester,	13, 28
Browne, Lord John,	30
Brundtland, Gro Harlem,	75
Burkett, Paul,	94
Buthelezi, Gatsha,	80

Callaghan, James, 24
Cameron, David, 63
Campaign to Protect Rural England, 45
Carbon trading, 34-7
Carbon footprint, 13, 48, 64
Carson, Rachel, 51
Chevron, 31
China, 20, 68, 69, 75
Climate change, 12, 34, 67-9
Clinton, Bill, 21, 69
Club of Rome, 13, 27, 37, 40
Congo, Democratic Republic, 40, 41
Connolly, James, 91
Crossrail, 18
Cuba, 76
Currie, Edwina, 52

Daumer, Georg Friedrich, 95
Davos, 21
Deforestation, 11
Developing world, 70-77
Disney Corporation, 19
Division of Labour, 62
'Downshifting', 60
Duffy, Michael, 45
Dunster, Bill, 64-5

EasyJet, 37, 55
Ecologist, 22, 27, 50
EcoSecurities, 35-6
Ehrlich, Paul, 11, 13
Eisenhower, Dwight, 25
Eliasch, John, 82
Energy, 21, 37-40, 63-5
English Heritage, 45

Enron,	15, 38-40, 69
Environmental Defence Fund,	74
'Ethical shopping',	48-51
European Union,	24, 35, 36, 43, 68, 69, 70, 76, 77
Evian,	49
'Externalities',	85-90
Exxon,	31
Fearnley-Whittingstall, Hugh,	24
Friedman, Milton,	85
Ford Motor Company,	15
Foster, John Bellamy,	94, 95
Fuel protestors,	88
Gaia thesis,	84
Galileo,	89
Ghana,	23
Genetically Modified Organisms (GMOs),	70
Germany,	70
Gilder, George,	16
Gingrich, Newt,	85
Girardet, Herbert,	11
Goldsmith, Edward,	22, 27
Goldsmith, Sir James,	15
Goldsmith, Sheherazade,	22
Goldsmith, Zac,	22, 28, 31, 32, 51, 53
Goodlife, The,	63
Gore, Albert,	21, 25, 36, 51, 69
'Green belt',	44-7
'Green revolution',	75
Greenpeace,	55, 63
'Greenwashing',	25-7
Guatemala,	79
Guthrie, Woody,	75

H. J. Heinz and Co.,	31
Haekel, Ernst,	84
Handy, Charles,	21
Hall, Sir Peter,	47
Harrod, Arthur Roy,	84
Hillhouse, David,	33
Hobson, John,	14
Housing,	44-7
HSBC,	26, 36
Icahn, Carl,	15
Iceland,	70
Imperial Chemicals Industries,	24, 31
Independent Whaling Commission,	70
India,	20, 23, 68, 69, 75
Indigenous peoples,	78-81
Intellectual property,	10, 19
International Panel on Climate Change (IPCC),	69
International Rivers Network,	74
Jacobs, Michael,	85, 92
Japan,	70
Johnson, Hewlett,	35
Juniper, Tony,	31, 53, 68
Keynesians,	86
King, Alexander,	27
King, Sir David,	9
Kyoto summit,	34, 68-9
Labour Party,	92
Lacey, Robert,	13, 52
Land,	40-47, 76, 81
Lay, Kenneth,	39-40
Leadbeater, Charles,	16, 20

Leggett, Jeremy,	23, 25, 36
Leisure time,	60
Lenin, Vladimir Ilyich,	79
Livingstone, Ken,	65, 85
Lloyd, Daniel,	89
Loch Lomond,	43
Lovelock, James,	84
Lovins, Amory,	37, 39-40
L'Oreal,	23, 25
Lucas, Caroline,	53
Marcos, Ferdinand,	80, 81
Martin, Chris,	53
McDonalds,	52
MacSharry, Ray,	43
Malthus, reverend Thomas,	8
Manchester University,	35
Maren, Michael,	11
Marx, Karl,	34, 93-6
Mashantucket Pequod,	81
Meadows, Dennis and Donella,	27
Melchett, Lord Peter,	24, 28, 31
Menchu, Rigoberta,	79
Meszaros, Istvan,	28
Mexico,	75
Mishan, E. J.,	85-90
Miskito Indians,	80
Mobil,	31
Monbiot, George,	29, 32, 53, 55
Mond, Alfred,	24
Monsanto,	22, 31
Morgan Stanley,	35
Morris, William,	91
Murdoch, Rupert,	25
Narmada Dam,	74

National Health Service, 18, 87
National Trust, 23
Naughton, John, 19
'Negawatts', 37-40
Neo-classical economics, 83-90
Nestlé, 30
New Forest, 43
New Economics Foundation 31, 65-6, 92
New Economy, 16, 20
Nixon, Richard, 28
Norway, 70
Non Governmental Organisations (NGOs), 70, 72, 74

Oil, 11
O'Leary, Michael, 54
Oliver, Jamie, 24
Organic food/farming 43, 48, 51-3
Oxburgh, Ronald, 30

Pacific Gas and Electricity, 37-9
Parkinson, Sara, 31
Pearce, Charles, 90
Peccei, Aurelio, 27
Perelman, Michael, 19
Peters, Tom, 21
Philip Morris 31
Pollan, Michael, 53
Porritt, Jonathan, 28, 31
Portland, 45
Private Finance Initiative, 18
Productivity, 58-9, 62

Reagan, Ronald, 81
Recycling, 61, 62
Reich, Robert, 16
Rio Tinto Zinc, 30

Robbins, Lionel,	83
Roddick, Anita,	23, 25
Rogers, Sir Richard,	46
Roosevelt, Franklin D.,	81
Ruskin, John,	27, 91
Sahlins, Marshall,	78
Sainsbury's,	24
Secrett, Charles,	29
Seldon, Arthur,	85, 86
Self-sufficiency,	62
Seminoles,	81
Shell (Anglo-Dutch Shell),	30, 35
Sinha, Ashok,	53
Silva, Alberto Caiero da,	56
Simm, Andrew,	92
'Smart growth'	44-7
Smith, Adam,	62, 83
Smith, Ian,	80
Smith, Margaret Laws,	27
Smithers, Alan,	15
Sobhan, Rehman,	10
'Social Darwinism',	84
Socialism,	91-6
Soil Association,	24, 53, 55
Solar Century/Solar Aid,	23
South Downs,	43
Spencer, Herbert,	84
Stoll, David,	79
Stern, Nicholas,	85
Suess, Eduard,	84
Survival International,	78
Swaminathan, M.S.,	75
Tansley, Arthur,	84
Tasaday,	80-1

Taxation,	87
Tesco,	24, 25, 26, 31, 57
Thatcher, Margaret,	63, 67, 90
Tickell, Sir Crispin,	67
Town and Country Planning Act,	47
Trading Emissions,	36
'Traffic calming',	59
Trotsky, Leon,	93, 96
Unemployment,	58
Unilever,	25
United Nations,	42, 75, 79
United States of America,	68, 69, 70, 77
Wal-Mart,	26
Wambugu, Florence,	76
'Washington consensus',	83
Wilson, Des,	31, 32
Wilson, Harold,	92
Working time,	58-60, 62
World Bank,	35, 41, 74, 83
World Wildlife Fund,	41
Worldwatch Institute,	8, 28
Yanomani,	82